DIRTY SECRETS

of the
World's Worst
Employee

Jenn Sadai

*If I can,
You can.*

Jan-Carol
Publishing, Inc

"every story needs a book"

Dirty Secrets of the World's Worst Employee
Jenn Sadai

Published September 2015
Express Editions
Imprint of Jan-Carol Publishing, Inc

ISBN: 978-1-939289-71-1
Library of Congress Control Number: 2015951727

You may contact the publisher:
Jan-Carol Publishing, Inc
PO Box 701
Johnson City, TN 37605
publisher@jancarolpublishing.com
jancarolpublishing.com

This book is dedicated to my Uncle Jeff for believing in my abilities as a writer and my good friend Heather Pajot for inspiring me to run a marathon. I wouldn't have this story to tell without both of you. The story of my crooked career is also dedicated to anyone who has encountered an unappreciative, inappropriate, or demanding boss over the course of their careers.

Letter to the Reader

Although this story is filled with true tales of bad behavior in the workplace, it is not my intent to make any person, or company, look corrupt. Businesses are run by people, people are not perfect, and therefore there will never be a perfect place to work.

Every company has its dirty secrets and changing jobs won't solve the problem. The key to surviving a world filled with corporate corruption and malicious managers is learning what you're willing to tolerate and what you're capable of changing. It's remembering that it's only a job and there will be always be other opportunities if it doesn't work out.

The roles we fill to earn a living do not define our impact on the world. How we interact with people is the real indicator of our character and capabilities. Everyone is trying to survive and thrive in a chaotic, materialistic world. There is no need to knock someone else down to get where you want to be. In the end, it's those who choose to lift and carry people along their way who are truly rewarded.

Turn your profession into a purpose. Look for ways to improve the daily grind for those around you. Be the person who brightens someone's day. Respect and appreciate your co-workers and you'll receive the same in return.

Wishing you extraordinary success,

Jenn Sadai

Acknowledgements

Special appreciation to Jan-Carol Publishing, Inc., Rob Sadai, Christine Boakes, Liz Cormier, Jeremy Boakes, Shawna Boakes, Rahel Levesque, Deb Birchard, Sarah Pinsonneault, Paula Michaluk, Kim Chapieski and Kim Harrison for their constant support and encouragement.

I would also like to thank Louise Smith Photography for taking my photo for the back cover and Kim Harrison for designing the front cover. Your impressive talents constantly amaze me.

My Crooked Career Path

Headed in the Right Direction

This is the story of my crooked career path. It's the unexpected and unusual route I took to find my true calling—writing. I was actually headed in the right direction early on in my life, but some unavoidable steps in the wrong direction eventually tossed me completely off course. Okay, that's somewhat of a cop-out.

Not every misstep was unavoidable, and some of the stumbles I've had in my career can only be blamed on my own inexperience. I already planned on sharing those gritty details throughout this story, so I might as well be honest right from the beginning.

I can now proudly admit that I made some entertaining and educational mistakes throughout my career, which in turn was the inspiration for writing this story. I feel confident that many others will relate to the workplace follies I've experienced and as always, I'm perfectly comfortable publishing my mistakes for the whole world's review and criticism. I really don't fear judgement or persecution, because I know that I'm not the only one who's behaved as, or at least felt like they were, the world's worst employee.

So, what's the worst thing you've ever done at a job?

1

Lie?

Steal?

Storm out, screaming obscenities?

Everyone has experienced career mishaps to varying degrees, and although I've never stormed out of a workplace screaming, I've been escorted out by my manager for calling the owner a bunch of nasty names in an emotionally-charged email. I've made mistakes, I've worked for companies that have made mistakes, and I'm sure that most people who chose to purchase a book entitled *Dirty Secrets of the World's Worst Employee* have also made a few mistakes in their career.

When you consider all of the professional catastrophes that have made the evening news, you can only imagine how many smaller-scale versions of Enron and WorldCom exist in today's society. Look at the poor decisions of Martha Stewart, Clarence Thomas, and Detroit's former Mayor, Kwame Kilpatrick. Have you ever wondered how many similar cases are being swept under the rug in your own city? We only heard about their indiscretions because they were already in the media spotlight.

I've seen my share of power hungry troublemakers and corporate corruption. I've witnessed interoffice affairs, sexual harassment, theft, bullying, and manipulation. I live in a relatively small Canadian city, and I've personally seen enough to know that every company has its own dirty secrets. Companies are run by people, and let's face it, people are not perfect.

Mistakes are an inevitable part of our fundamental learning process. That's why it is necessary to accept and reflect on our bad decisions we've made. Analyzing our previous errors in judgment allow us to evolve and improve our decision making process. I am not ashamed to put any of the embarrassing, foolish, or deceitful things I've done in writing. I want people to learn from my poor choices, and feel better about their own dirty deeds.

However, it is unfair of me to put the mistakes of others in writing without their written consent. That's why I've changed insignificant details, physical descriptions, and people's names. I want to protect the innocent, as well as the not-so-innocent. This is my story.

It is my unique tale of a turbulent and triumphant journey towards finding my place in the workforce. It is no one else's journey. I did what I could to protect people's identities, because I truly wish no ill will on anyone in this novel. Their mistakes aren't any worse than my own. I do not have any judgment on the bad choices of others. If you've read my first book, *Dark Confessions of an Extraordinary, Ordinary Woman*, you would instantly understand why I won't condemn the mistakes of others.

My list of past poor decisions is longer than this novel. I'm not criminal or evil, but I'm flawed. Emotions have clouded my better judgment at times, in both my personal and professional life. I'm pretty sure I'm not the world's worst employee—although I've been made to feel that way at times.

That feeling of inferiority was the second inspiration for this novel. I am certain I'm not the only one who has had the pleasure of dealing with an unappreciative manager or an infuriating boss who made them feel useless and unappreciated. That is why I felt it was necessary to publish my story of struggling to find real success in a professional work environment. I wasted several years of my career doubting and discounting my abilities and potential because of a careless mistake or two.

The fact that I'm not perfect shouldn't prevent my dreams from coming true. Past mistakes don't deem me unworthy of a good career. My life may not have gone exactly how I planned it, but that doesn't mean I should just stop trying to create the life I truly want.

As a young and naïve child, I was convinced I would be a famous writer. I started writing poetry and short stories when I was in grade school, and my passion for writing continued until I was in my early twenties. My family, friends, and teachers encouraged me to write and insisted I had a natural talent throughout my childhood.

I expressed everything I was feeling with a pen and a notebook—this was obviously a long time ago, way back in the pre-laptop era. I was shy and insecure in my daily life, yet confident and passionate on paper.

At age thirteen, I was given the honor of attending a writer's workshop taught by a Canadian author, Welwyn Wilton Katz. Everyone in the class wrote a short story as part of the workshop, and the library that hosted it decided to bundle everyone's short stories together in a pink, spiral-bound book. All of my family members bought a copy, and I was thrilled to share a story that came from my imagination with my loved ones.

It wasn't a great story. I now cringe at my lack of creativity, but it was pretty insightful for someone who had barely experienced any of the challenges that come with growing up in the real world. I was on the right career path early on in my life, and even had a job writing advertising copy for local businesses within a year of graduating college.

Life takes you places you never thought you'd go.

How I became a marketing assistant at a department store and then a food and beverage manager in my early thirties is a long and complex story. My career has taken many unexpected turns, and I had no idea that I was on the right path all along. If I hadn't endured my tragic career history, I wouldn't have written my first book or have this unusual and inspiring story to tell. I also would not have been blessed with the same amazing support group. I met many of the best people in my life at some of the worst jobs imaginable.

My crooked career path started at the innocent and impressionable age of fourteen. Like most teenagers, my first real work experiences were in the food service industry. I answered phones at a pizzeria two nights a week and then picked up a second job, providing cheerful customer service in the food court at one of the local malls.

Sadly, I learned early on in life that having a boss was often more challenging than the job itself. My first boss was a man in his fifties who would repeatedly, "accidentally" rub his hand across my butt when I was washing dishes in the sink at the end of my shift. He made countless sexual comments towards me, despite the fact that I was young enough to be his granddaughter.

"You should wear a bikini and dance on the counter. It will help attract more business."

I should have stood up for myself, or at least told my parents about his suggestive behavior. I knew he was being inappropriate, and that it should have made me feel more uncomfortable than it did. However, I rationalized his behavior as being relatively harmless. He was old and physically weak. If he ever went too far, I was confident I could defend myself. Plus, I secretly got him back for his dirty old man behavior. I kept my mouth shut when I discovered that the delivery drivers had a pretty smart system for stealing money from him.

I may not have said anything about my boss' shameful behavior when I was teenager, but I would never allow that to happen now. I'd like to think that I've finally mastered the art of gentle rejection and correction. It's pretty sad that I've experienced sexual harassment often enough in the workplace that I felt the need to develop a strategy and coping mechanism.

I'm definitely not the only one. It's quite frightening how many men in the workplace will make disrespectful comments or attempt unwanted physical contact without giving it a second thought. I've met very few men who treat me as an equal in the workplace, but I'll cover that necessary topic later on.

The job at the pizzeria had its perks and faults, just like every other job I've had since. The benefits were that it was incredibly close to my house, the work itself was easy, and they only needed me seven hours a week. I was normally off work by 8pm, so I could still do things with my friends after work. Several people from my high school worked there, including one of my closest friends, which made it feel more like a social hangout than a job. It also came with the added bonus of making a little extra money in tips.

I always loved leaving work with cash in my hands.

I've been saving jars of loose change since my first job at the pizzeria. When I was younger, I had a different jar for each denomination, although now I just toss it all together in an old coffee tin. My change jars used to be my savings account and I saved up over $800 by the time I finished high school, which was later used to buy my college textbooks. I picked up this useful habit from my favorite uncle. My Uncle Jeff would bring a massive water jug—the kind used with a watercooler—filled to the rim with coins to my dad's house every Christmas. He would let his nieces and nephews keep whatever they rolled during his visit.

I earned better cash tips at the customer service position in the food court at the mall, but it was a forty-five minute bus ride for a three or four hour shift. I had to hop on a bus right after I finished school, which made for an exceptionally long and draining day.

I was lucky that my mom would pick me up after work, otherwise it wouldn't have been worth the paycheck. I usually didn't finish work until 9pm, and it wasn't really safe to take the bus home at night by myself. In all honesty, I live in a pretty safe city and I'm sure I would have been fine. But my mom insisted it wasn't safe, and I wasn't going to turn down a free and convenient ride home.

I've had a significant number of jobs in my short life and I've only had a few decent bosses or supervisors. I've met amazing co-workers, great business owners, and one incredible general manager, but very few good bosses.

I think that's because shit trickles down.

They get pressure from their bosses and pass it on down to the subordinates. I'm sure most managers try to be good to their employees, but they're human and are allowed to lose their patience from time to time. Eventually, almost every boss will do something inappropriate, ignorant, or unfair. I hate to be cynical, but it's the nature of the modern business world.

Unfortunately for me, the undereducated and overly arrogant fast food supervisor at my other job was a perfect example of shit trickling down. Patrick's entire role consisted of telling me and the other employees what to do. It didn't matter how busy we got or how much needed to be prepped or cleaned. He would let us know what needed to be done, then hide in his tiny office where he talked on the phone with his girlfriend all night long.

Patrick was my second example of what it meant to be a boss and he showed me his own version of unacceptable boss behavior. He once asked me to pick up a mouse trap with a dead mouse on it. I told him I wasn't comfortable doing it and that I had a weak stomach, but he insisted it was part of my job. I repeatedly gagged before I even got within a few feet of it. I seriously thought I was going to throw up before I even got close to it, but I held it together enough to quickly sweep it into a dustpan and dump it into the garbage pail without getting physically sick.

My mother witnessed what happened because she was picking me up from work, and fortunately told me that it was okay to quit the job immediately following that stomach-churning incident. I still had the job at the pizzeria, and I was a full-time high school student. I didn't need to pick up dead mice for minimum wage.

Luckily, I went from the customer service position at the mall to becoming a waitress at a local golf course where my aunt worked. I didn't know it at the time, but it was the start of a long and mostly rewarding history of working at a variety of different golf courses throughout Windsor-Essex County.

That simple waitressing job was one of the few jobs I truly loved.

There is a stigma about serving people for a living that I've never understood. It's a tough job that takes more skill than people realize. It's also very profitable. I truly enjoy serving others, and I made great tips for doing it. I was lucky to take home $20 a night at the pizzeria, but a good shift at the golf course earned me anywhere from $50-$100 in tips. I was making a lot more money per hour waitressing, so it didn't take me very long to quit the pizzeria—and my frisky boss—even though it was a convenient and easy way to earn a few extra bucks. I was almost eighteen, and ready to move on to more lucrative ways to earn a living.

My new place of employment was a public golf course that was only busy enough to need me if they were hosting a tournament, holiday buffet, baby/bridal shower, or some other similar family-type gatherings. The restaurant had regulars for brunch and buffet dinners, but the career servers with more seniority were always given those shifts first.

Waitressing at this public golf course was where I met one of my closest and lifelong friends, Rachel. She's an honest and rebellious tomboy just like me, plus we share many of the same bad habits. We hit it off instantly, and came up with a clever way to scam plates full of delicious buffet fare whenever we worked together.

The golf course had a behind-the-scenes access ramp and hallway that we would carry the food through before serving it. It was the only way to get the food down to the halls on the lower level. Every time we served a buffet in one of the downstairs banquet halls, we would stop and fix ourselves a plate in the secluded concrete hallway, before serving the paying clientele. We bonded over Swedish meatballs and penne.

Yes, I stole food from my employer. Not only will I guarantee that I'm not the only one who has done this terrible deed, but I doubt there is any waiter or waitress who hasn't snuck a fry or two when no one was looking, or grabbed some finger food from the walk-in fridge. As a server, you're surrounded by amazing food at all times. You'd have to be a saint to consistently resist the temptation. I'm sure I share this dirty little secret with the majority of people who have worked in a kitchen.

Creating a Path with a Purpose

A round the same time that I started the job at the golf course, I decided it was time to look for more professional work. I was about to be finished with high school, and my guidance counselor had recommended a career in marketing. She pointed out that there aren't many paying positions for writers in Windsor, and copywriting would open up a broader job market. It sounded exciting and fit within my skill set.

Like most idealistic young adults, I had big goals for my life and felt confident that I could easily achieve them by utilizing my strong work ethic and positive attitude. I was eager to take control of my future, so I wrote a compelling letter about my passion for copywriting and advertising, created a short survey, and then mailed it to every marketing-related business and advertising agency within a fifty mile radius.

The letter was asking for an opportunity to volunteer at their business and the survey contained questions about the marketing and advertising industry, as well as whether I should attend college or university. I received several responses to the survey, and a small, local advertising agency allowed me the privilege of volunteering at their office.

This was a pretty impressive accomplishment for someone who had only recently graduated high school. I was only eighteen and I already had my foot in the door of a real advertising agency. I sat in on production meetings, took detailed notes, made photocopies, and mentored under the tutelage of the experienced owner. He had successfully run the ad agency for over twenty years. I felt so fortunate to have such a remarkable career opportunity at such a young age, and proud that I was the one responsible for making it happen.

Henry Cole was one of the few respectable bosses I've had throughout my career. I remember him knowing everything there was to know about local businesses, local marketing campaigns, and how to create effective copywriting. His office was filled with trade magazines, and he read them cover to cover. I could also tell that he sincerely cherished imparting his wisdom to me. Unlike my previous employment, Henry never asked me to do anything degrading or disgusting.

However, he was demanding and an extreme perfectionist.

You'll notice throughout this book that I have a strange history of suddenly stumbling into seemingly perfect jobs that later turn into an ugly mess or a tragic nightmare. The pizza place was the first place I ever applied for a job, and it was located two houses down the street from where I lived. I assumed I lucked out because I was hired by the first person who saw my resume and it was only a two minute walk to work. As I got older, my boss' comments became more offensive, the money really wasn't worth it, and it was no longer the ideal place to work.

Every job seems great in the beginning.

Volunteering at the ad agency was exhilarating and educational, but working for free was less than ideal. I made some money at the waitressing job at the golf course, but it was only five to ten hours on the weekend and I wanted to move into an apartment with my boyfriend as quickly as possible. I desperately needed to start making real money.

Every time I've needed to make a career change, things magically come together for me. I know I can't be the only one who's experienced this phenomenon, and I imagine a seamless shuffle from one opportunity to the next is quite common. I couldn't tell you if it's a result of the cosmic plan of the universe, good karma, or the simple cliché that when one door closes, another will always open. I've just always felt like my career path had a mind of its own, and I was just along for the ride.

This was one of those unplanned moments in my life when circumstances and good timing showed me where I was headed next. A few weeks after I started volunteering, the bookkeeper/secretary at the ad agency quit and I was offered her position. Unexpectedly, the woman whose shoes I would be filling warned me that I would hate the position before she left. Of course I didn't pay any attention to her advice.

I wasn't even willing to consider that the job would have any flaws. I was so honored and excited to be offered such a rewarding opportunity at a real, professional company. I had not even begun my business marketing program at college and I was already getting real world experience. This was a huge leap in the right direction.

Henry was exceptionally considerate and willing to work around the golf course's schedule. Even after I started college, he allowed me to come in whenever I had spare time. I was mostly responsible for the filing, invoicing, and bookkeeping, which could be done after normal business hours. I tried to work as much during the day as possible, because I loved the atmosphere.

The energy in a fast-paced ad agency can be electric. My dream of becoming a writer was quickly shifting to becoming a copywriter and the owner of a trendy ad agency. Melrose Place was one of my favorite shows at the time and I idolized Heather Locklear's character, Amanda Woodward. She was a fierce advertising executive who demanded and received respect.

I also wanted to follow in my new boss' footsteps. I loved the feeling of being part of a real office, especially one that thrived on creativity and catchy slogans. I bought classy high heels and business suits, learned everything I could, and loved every minute of it.

In hindsight, my first professional job was too good to be true, but at this point in the story, it felt like I landed my dream job. Many drastic changes and challenges were going on in my personal life while I was working at the ad agency, and I ended up making a hasty decision to move into an apartment with my boyfriend before either of us were financially ready.

Despite working two jobs, the only way we could afford to live on our own was managing the apartment building we lived in exchange for free rent. My mother's boyfriend's father owned an apartment complex, so they took a chance on letting me and my boyfriend manage it, even though we were not qualified to do so. We had no idea what a massive undertaking we were accepting at the time. I soon discovered free rent came at a very high price.

The apartment building only had ten units, but it felt like there was always a vacancy we were trying to fill, an apartment that needed repairs, or a tenant that was behind on their rent. It was located in a less-than-affluent area of the city and attracted petty crooks, heavy drinkers, hoarders, and a crazy cat lady who vanished less than three months after she moved in. She left everything she had in her apartment, including seven cats, and three months' worth of cat feces. The smell was what tipped us off that she was no longer living there.

No human being could live with that smell.

Now imagine being the one who had to clean it up. I gagged a whole lot worse cleaning her apartment that day than I did when I picked up the dead mouse at the mall. Managing that apartment building was filled with many unpleasant tasks, which is probably the reason why we only lasted a year in that role.

One task in particular was so horrendous that I knew I had no choice other than to find a new place to live, although now it's just a funny story I tell. We had to bring the trash bins to the road, once a week on garbage day. Yes, it would seem easy enough and my boyfriend, Shane, was the one who usually did it. I'm an independent woman; however, I'm fine with leaving trash removal to the man of the house. Shane did very little to help manage that apartment building, so I made him responsible for moving the smelly trash bins.

Unfortunately for me, I noticed one evening that he forgot to put them at the curb. I knew garbage collection would take place really early the following morning. Shane wasn't home and wouldn't be back until much later, so I decided to drag the containers to the road by myself. As I said, I didn't think it would be very difficult to do. However, when I grabbed the first garbage bin, a giant rat jumped out at me, landed on my chest, fell off, and then scurried away.

I dropped the garbage bin like it was on fire and ran.

Picture my arms flying wildly in the air while I screamed at the top of my lungs as I ran for several blocks without slowing down. People came out of their houses to make sure no one was being brutally murdered.

I've never been so frightened and grossed out in my life. I swear the rat that landed on me was the size of a cat, although no one believes me. I didn't really get a close look at it because I was too busy running for my life to look back, so I won't actually insist it was the world's biggest rat. Nevertheless, in the light of day, with Shane's help, we moved the garbage containers and found massive holes dug in the ground underneath where the bins were kept. The holes were big enough to fit several plump cats.

After that horrific incident, I became obsessed with killing the rats. I'll admit, it wasn't a very attractive side of me. At first, I just poured a little rat poison in the holes and filled them in with dirt and gravel. Unfortunately, there were new holes by the next morning.

So, I dumped poisonous chemicals all over the dirt underneath and around the bins, poured the best rat poison money could buy into the holes, and then filled them in with large rocks. There were new holes within a few days. It must have been a breed of mutant super rats, because nothing I tried worked. We eventually gave up the landlord gig and found a new place to rent far, far away from my disgusting enemies. This was the second time that rodents interfered with my employment.

Managing the apartment building, waitressing at the golf course, working part-time hours at the advertising agency, and my college program had me stretched pretty thin. Thankfully, I was determined to succeed and willing to sacrifice sleep and my social life to make it work.

Back then I was still young enough to function relatively well on only four or five hours of sleep each night. I doubt I could manage that same crazy schedule now, although I did end up with a singular job later on in my career that came pretty close to same amount of hours. But we'll get to that crucial learning experience later on in this story.

From age eighteen to twenty, I was able to somehow be everywhere I needed to be when I needed to be there. I was doing quite well juggling my responsibilities, although my college courses suffered somewhat. Some days

I was skipping classes to work at the ad agency because I needed money, and other times I missed the in-class lessons to play countless games of Euchre in the cafeteria with my new college friends.

I worked almost every night and weekend, so college was my only chance to have a little fun with my friends. I still passed all of my courses, but I didn't achieve my usual high academic standards. Thankfully my career was already headed in the right direction. I didn't need to be at the top of my class to land a great job. I already had one, and it was about to become even more impressive.

Once again, I was simply in the right place at the right time.

I'd apologize for my excessive use of clichés, but there's a reason these classic sayings are repeated time after time. They're universal truths. I received criticism for using clichés in my first book and debated removing them from this story, but I don't see any value in rewriting a sentence that already accurately sums up a perspective.

My stories are not flowery tales used to capture the imagination and whisk readers away to a fantasy land. They are real experiences that I am sharing to inform and reassure others who have faced similar obstacles in their own lives. I am perfectly comfortable using the cliché "I was in the right place at the right time", because that's the truth.

Around the same time I graduated from college, the production manager at the advertising agency decided to quit working there to further her education. Strangely, I received the same type of warning as I had from the bookkeeper two years prior. The production manager never came out and said it directly to me, but her body language and training told a different story.

I already knew she was partially leaving the agency due to stress, because of the high demands of our strict boss. At that time, I was foolish enough to think that it was her who couldn't handle the pressure, rather than considering that the pressure of the job was unmanageable. I had no personal history of my boss and mentor being too demanding, so I leapt at the opportunity.

Prior to finishing my last semester of college, my work schedule was spread out to accommodate my daytime classes. I would go in early in the morning or late at night to distribute any mail, enter any invoices in the bookkeeper software program, print checks, type notes, and catch up on the filing.

I didn't have much interaction with my boss. If he worked late, which he did more often than not, his door was usually closed. So of course I said yes when he offered me her position. I was only twenty, and had already landed an extraordinary position with an established company in my intended field. I couldn't ask for or expect anything more. So, I quit waitressing at the golf course and prepared myself for my new professional career.

Over the next two weeks, the production manager trained me on our clients, our suppliers, and how to quote print media. It was a lot to learn, and she spent most of the time warning me that our boss was very particular and didn't tolerate errors. It seemed like she couldn't stress it enough, and it was making me feel a little uneasy.

As soon as she left, I was expected to manage all of her responsibilities. Unfortunately, I wasn't exactly handed her title or salary. My boss felt I was too young and inexperienced for the title of production manager, so he changed the job title to project coordinator. I couldn't argue with my complete lack of experience.

I was fresh out of college and in charge of making sure all of our suppliers fulfilled every one of our client's marketing needs, to their exact specification. There were usually between fifteen to twenty projects on the go and crucial details that needed to be 100 percent accurate. I was accurate most of the time, but I am human.

I quickly learned that my boss expected perfection from himself and his staff. The more he demanded flawless performance out of me, the more mistakes I ended up making. I was also still managing the bookkeeper and secretarial duties for the agency, so I was working at least fifty hours a week trying to stay on top of everything.

I was starting to see why the previous bookkeeper and production manager both quit so suddenly. Henry never said anything inappropriate, but he made me feel like a failure over the smallest errors. In retrospect, he would have been an even greater teacher for me if I had been in a more stable and confident place in my personal life. Unfortunately, it was too much negativity for me to handle without it having an effect on my self-esteem and proficiency at work.

After working for him for one year as his full-time project coordinator and bookkeeper, I decided it was time for me to move on. It was a difficult decision, and I must admit I was terrified to leave my first real professional job. Plus I felt guilty that I was searching for a new job behind my boss's back, because I sincerely appreciated the knowledge and professional advice I had received from him over the past three years.

How many people have looked for a new job on company time?

I know I'm not the only one who's done it, but I still felt bad about it. In reality, it's often a necessity; I know many employees who've searched for a new job during company hours. I felt bad because I gained an abundance of firsthand advertising experience, and it only happened because he took the time to respond to my survey. He took a chance on me when I had no experience or qualifications.

I felt indebted to him more than to myself.

I know how crazy that sounds, since no employer should be viewed as a greater priority than one's own happiness. I imagine I'm not the only one who stayed in a job because they felt they owed it to the company. Reality check—we owe it to ourselves to find careers that fulfill us.

Strangely, I still feel awkward when I see him, because I feel like I disappointed him. Luckily the guilt wasn't strong enough to keep me there very long, because I was destined to go down a different career path. I wouldn't be writing this book right now if I'd stayed there as his loyal employee forever. That wouldn't have made a very interesting storyline.

I may have felt indebted to him for giving me such a wonderful learning opportunity, but I knew his demanding nature was not something I could deal with on a long-term basis. I also realized there was no real opportunity for me to move up in the company. The ad agency consisted of three people; my boss (who was the only copywriter), the graphic design artist who had been there fifteen years, and myself. They were planning to merge with another company, but I looked into their current staff and everyone in that company had more experience than I did. I was getting the impression that the merger was going to bump me back down to being only a bookkeeper/receptionist. I went into marketing to become a copy-writer, which I didn't feel would ever be a feasible opportunity for me at that agency.

It was time to start a new adventure.

It's been said to me before that standing still stifles growth. Fortu-nately, my professional career was destined not to be stagnant and I grew along with it. When I was only twenty-one years old, I came up with a fifteen-year plan to gather a broad scope of marketing and advertising expe-rience and then open my own ad agency by the time I was thirty-three.

The plan was actually based on the number three. I already had three years working at an ad agency, so all I needed was three years selling adver-tising locally, three years as a junior copywriter in a large city like Toronto, three years as a senior copywriter for a large company, and three years as a manager within a large ad agency. That would give me the knowledge and knowhow I needed to manage a world-class agency on my own. I was a big dreamer who had high hopes for her career.

Of course, life never goes according to plan.

Tapping into
My Talent

I started off on the right foot and was fortunate to quickly land a position that suited my fifteen year plan. Or maybe I got this job first, and then developed my fifteen year plan? It was fourteen years ago and it makes more sense that I was hired for a position selling advertising, and then decided it would be the second step in my plan. I'm not psychic, or lucky enough to establish a specific job that will best suit my future and then suddenly land in it. This isn't a fictional tale, after all.

Either way, I was thrilled to test my abilities in the more social and independent side of advertising; magazine ad sales. A local business magazine had a position available for an account executive and I impressed the owner with my enthusiasm. Since my title was going to have the word executive in it, I thought it would be a positive step in the right direction. Job titles meant a lot to me in the start of my career.

Sadly, my current boss was not really pleased with my decision to leave his agency. Henry's reaction to the news validated my guilt. He had invested three years in developing my capabilities and felt I was abandoning him before he reaped the rewards of his teachings. He insisted I wasn't ready for a more challenging role, and that I still had a long way to go before I would reach his standards of perfectionism. Henry even tried to talk me out of taking it. Our relationship changed instantly, and my last two weeks were filled with many uncomfortable silences.

To soften the blow of my departure, I wrote a cute (cheesy) poem about how much more to life there was then work and left it in our conference room with a cardboard cut-out of myself. I now realize how childish, ridiculous, and embarrassing it was do that, but I have a long history of similar silliness and I've learned to be proud of my unusual quirkiness. It's always my goal to leave a lasting impression. As previously stated, I'm more confident on paper, so the poem was my chance to say what I really thought.

What most people won't realize—unless they're reading this book—is that I had truly good intentions when I decided to leave that poem. My boss was a workaholic whose wife used to complain to me that she never saw him. She would call me to find out how he was doing, because he was usually too busy to talk to her. This was my attempt to leave him with some good advice, since I was grateful for all of the business advice he shared with me. His life revolved around the agency and despite my young age, I already knew there was more to life than business. Oddly, I forgot that lesson later on in my career.

I remember being very excited about starting a new job, as well as incredibly nervous. I was eager to impress my new boss, and I had no idea if I would make a good salesperson. The position had an hourly rate that was almost the same as what I made as a project coordinator, but I could earn a lot more money in commission if I was able to successfully convince local businesses to run ads in the magazine. I'm outgoing, but not aggressive or pushy, and I knew that weakness could count against me in a sales environment.

I was a bundle of nerves and energy when I sat down at my new desk for the first time. I was no longer sitting in a lobby at a receptionist's desk. I now had my own cubicle! My new boss told me what territory I would be covering, and he gave me a copy of their advertising rates. He also left me with some past issues of the magazine and a phone book for reference material, so I could start booking appointments with potential clients. He gave me the tools I needed to be successful. It was up to me to figure out the best way to achieve my targets.

However, within ten minutes of him leaving me at my desk, I ripped my ankle-length skirt to the waistline. Yes, God has a funny sense of humor.

I was wearing a long, grey skirt, with a slit in the back that went up to my knees. I crossed my legs in the chair, but the hem of the skirt was stuck under the chair's wheel. I heard a frightening tearing sound as the skirt was torn straight up my backside to the waistband. My chubby white butt—only covered by a practically invisible thong—was completely exposed.

I was instantly mortified. Panic overwhelmed me, as I pondered how I could successfully get out of this situation without being totally humiliated at my brand new job. My desk was at the very back of a long, narrow office lined with occupied cubicles and I needed a way to get out without being seen. I also needed a legitimate excuse to leave my new job so suddenly. Thankfully, all my years as a sneaky teenager paid off and I was able to quickly come up with an excuse and an escape plan.

I faked a phone call to a potential client and acted like I already booked a sales appointment. I then grabbed the large leather briefcase my brother bought me and held it behind me to cover my ass, as I quickly scurried out the door. No one in the office said anything about it, so I'm pretty sure I miraculously escaped the utter humiliation of the people I just started working with seeing my bare butt.

Although I didn't start my career at the magazine with an uncomfortable scene going on public record, I've willingly and almost proudly retold that story countless times to some of the very same co-workers. I am not above telling a mortifying story about myself to make people laugh. I feel the same way about that as I do about sharing my past mistakes. I'm just relieved no one actually saw my chubby white bum.

I can handle a little embarrassment if it benefits others.

My tales of work faux-pas are so legendary that they were the original inspiration for this book. I went to a party once and was introduced as "the girl who sent her boss an email calling him an ego-testical, short Italian prick." My insane mishaps and entertaining bad luck were hot topics that were certainly worth exploring.

For me, this book became more than just a funny tale of finding your way in the world. It is filled with shocking scandals, corporate greed, and bosses who should be locked up for their criminal behavior. The title of this book is somewhat sarcastic, since I ended up being a good employee at most of the places I've worked. However, at this point in my story, I could have easily transitioned into one of the world's worst employees.

Sales gave me freedom for the first time in my professional career. I went from working fifty hours a week, chained to a desk staring at a computer screen, to only working forty hours a week, which were mainly spent visiting a wide variety of businesses all over Windsor and Essex County. I could do what I wanted, when I wanted, as long as the clients were happy and the magazine was full of paying ads. Lucky for me, this task wasn't as time-consuming as my boss assumed.

I was a horrible, yet successful employee.

To counteract my inability to push or aggressively persuade companies into buying ads, I tapped into my marketing skills and copywriting talents. I would create compelling ads for clients before they signed the contract. I would research their business and then develop a personalized magazine ad that was too good for them to resist.

It would just be a rough sketch, but the caption and catch phrase would usually be enough to sway their decision. I was able to consistently create clever ad copy that captured their business's main objective. I don't want to brag, especially since I have no clue where these ideas came from (thank you God), but I would just be sitting there and unique copy would pop into my head. It's the same thing that happens when I work on my books or poetry.

Once again, thank you God.

If the rough sketch I drew didn't instantly sell the client on the ad space, I'd enlist the services of the magazine's talented graphic design artist, Kya. She had this amazing ability; she could transform my sloppy sketches into works of art. In fact, she is the talented artist who designed both of my book covers. Her artistic ability was her gift from God, and she was also using it to make a living. I believe wholeheartedly that everyone has an innate talent, and they owe it to themselves to pursue that talent.

Almost 90 percent of the time, the client would love the ad concept so much that they would sign on to the magazine for at least three months. Eventually, I had enough repeat business that I just needed to continue creating new ads to keep my clients satisfied. I would often stress to them the importance of using a consistent theme, so the ad wouldn't require that much changing.

My ability to quickly fill ad space and efficiently handle clients' accounts allotted me a considerable amount of spare time. Since I was allowed to come and go from the office without question, I would spend my free time running errands, stopping by my apartment to do chores or watch a little television, or sometimes playing bingo with my friend Shelley.

I met Shelley in college and ended up recommending her for a sales position at the town newspaper, owned by the same company as the magazine. She was one of my closest friends and we were already used to spending a lot of time together. She was also insanely lucky at bingo and would generously split her winnings with me.

Shelley was a super saleswoman. She used her charm, positive attitude, and strong customer service skills to quickly prove she was worthy of the endorsement. Working with Shelley was an added bonus to a job I already loved. I felt certain it wouldn't be that hard to last three years in this position, and then move onto a junior copywriting position at a bigger company. I had freedom, a decent paycheck, the opportunity to write ad copy, and the chance to work with fun people like Kya and Shelley. My fifteen-year plan seemed to be going better than I could have imagined.

As I've learned over the course of my ever-changing professional history, all good things must come to an end, and this fabulous job wasn't any different. Although I could picture myself staying with the company for several years and fulfilling my fifteen-year career plan, circumstances decided to speed up my agenda.

After I enjoyed about a year of my career being the most positive aspect of my life, things came crashing down pretty hard in both my personal and professional life. It started with my friend Shelley being impregnated by an unworthy suitor, who immediately abandoned her and his responsibilities. She was already a single mother of two, and struggling to stay afloat financially.

For those who've read the other half of my journey—*Dark Confessions of an Extraordinary, Ordinary Woman*—I don't need to explain how this part of my story ends. Shelley made a poor decision, in what she felt was the best interests of her children. I've decided not to rehash the details out of respect for her. Financial burdens clouded her judgment, and it temporarily cost us our friendship. I've forgiven and forgotten her mistake. Our friendship was reinstated several years ago, because I know how easy it is to made bad decisions during times of struggle. I've made many in my life.

The rapid decline in the job's appeal was amplified by the existing editor (who was another friend of mine) leaving the magazine and being replaced by a bitter woman whom I couldn't seem to win over. You could tell she was unhappy with her personal life, and driven to make others just as miserable.

It was the receptionist and new editor who eventually drove me out in tears. They started disgusting rumors about Shelley and me, accused me of being involved in her mistake, and even framed me for something completely different. One of them deleted the current issue of the magazine from the computer, and then accused me of doing it. Fortunately, my boss had physical evidence that proved my innocence. The file was deleted at a time when only my boss and the receptionist had been in the building. This was my first experience with the cruel, cutthroat world of modern business, but it wouldn't be my last.

I felt it was necessary for me to move on from the magazine, for my own sanity. After several uncomfortable and stressful months where I was being accused of unethical acts that I hadn't committed, combined with secret guilt for the company's time I did waste at bingo and the fact that I was slowly building a side business on company time, was more than I could handle emotionally. It didn't matter that my co-workers accused me of things I didn't do, because I knew I wasn't actually a loyal employee.

A Huge Leap Forward

This was my first big leap of faith.

I'm somewhat foolish when it comes to taking risks. I dream big and worry later. I decided at the incredibly young age of twenty-three to open a home-based advertising agency with my talented friend, Kya. Our clients from the magazine were asking us to design business cards, logos, brochures, and other advertising material, because they loved the inventive ads we were creating for the magazine. We already had clientele, so starting an advertising agency seemed like the next logical step in my career.

Kya was getting married in a few months and couldn't afford to leave the magazine, but she could still do the graphic design work at home in the evening. I would make sales calls during the day and she would create the masterpieces at night. We were a great team!

I was now planning to attempt my fifteen-year career goal after only 4½ years in the industry. I can see now that I was not ready for it, but twelve years ago I leaped without looking

There was a reason I'd mapped out a fifteen-year plan in the first place. It was the influence of my boss at the ad agency. Henry Cole stressed that preparation, experience, and attention to detail were crucial to his success. I wasn't paying attention to the fact that I skipped the preparation and experience aspect, jumping right into running an ad agency.

Our agency had a promising start, but we were only profiting a few hundred dollars each—monthly—and I couldn't live off that. It was not enough to cover my credit card payments, and I still needed to eat and put gas in my car. I had to secure a more stable income to ensure I didn't starve, so I went back to waitressing at a golf course. However, this course was not as busy and didn't have a banquet hall, so I still wasn't making enough to cover my financial needs and had to pick up a third part-time job. Once again, I was trying to balance too many jobs and something was destined to fall.

When I first started at this golf course, the restaurant had a really good manager and I honestly liked the job. The manager and waitstaff were mostly attractive party girls, which suited that time in my life—the only time I've been single as an adult. Unfortunately, the supportive and encouraging manager ending up quitting shortly after being hired, and they replaced her with an overweight career waitress who didn't appreciate the more physically appealing servers taking away all of her customers.

She fired us off one by one.

I was the last person to be forced out, because I was one of the oldest and possibly the least attractive. I never gave her any reason to fire me, so she had to be creative. My new manager gave me only one shift on the schedule and it was at the exact same time as my other job. She knew I was unavailable Tuesday afternoons, and implied that she would continue to give me that as my only shift. It wasn't a busy shift and not worth fighting to stay, especially since I still had the business and the other side job a few hours a week; the reason I couldn't work Tuesdays.

Fortunately, when she forced me out six months later, I was able to pick up extra hours at job number three. To help pay off the massive debt I accumulated with my ex-boyfriend, I accepted a part-time position serving food in the cafeteria at a tool and mold shop where my mother worked. It was a tiny kitchen in a dirty shop, serving mediocre food to large groups of hungry men simultaneously. They could only offer me ten to fifteen hours a week, but it was enough to cover my food expenses, especially since I was also able to eat for free while I was working.

Free food is my favorite job perk.

The head cook was really nice and it was a relatively easy job, except for rushing around the thirty minutes before and after the lunch bell went off. Everyone took break at the same time, which meant we had to prepare twenty to fifty meals to be ready within a few minutes of each other. It was only me and the head cook, but we managed to make it happen each and every time. I guarantee most of the food was cold, but the guys never complained.

I truly believe that every job I've had along the way was necessary for my future happiness. Each job filled in a piece of my puzzle. Surprisingly, that lower-level, cafeteria position at a tool and mold shop was the most essential step in the right direction.

That was where I met my absolutely wonderful husband.

I started there in March and he was just a nice guy who would chat with me at the counter. I had just left my abusive ex, and I wasn't really in a hurry to replace him. It was during a wild time in my life and William seemed to be a clean cut and well-mannered man. I never pictured myself with a well-behaved, law-abiding man. I didn't feel deserving of a good guy at that time in my life.

The only guys I thought were interested in me were the ones who would make sexual remarks and blatantly hit on me. I've always been oblivious to subtle come-ons. I have inadvertently led on several men throughout my life because I didn't clue in that their kind gestures were actually expressions of interest.

Between the golf course and the factory filled with men, I was getting used to receiving a lot of attention from the opposite sex. That's why it seemed like a no-brainer to replace the golf course with a job driving a food truck to various industrial shops throughout the city. My main clientele were hungry men, most of which hadn't seen a woman all day. I intentionally seduced them and wore tight shirts and short shorts to boost my tips. I looked pretty enticing when I was twenty-four.

The woman I am now is surprisingly impressed with the decision I made then. I looked good and had the guts to show it off. I used men's weakness to increase my earnings. Some women may think that type of behavior makes women look trashy, but I have the right to dress however I feel comfortable. I felt it was appropriate for the environment I was working in at the time, and have no regrets. Men are going to ogle us regardless of what we are wearing, so why shouldn't I earn a little extra for having to put up with it?

Despite the fistful of cash I was making each day, I knew I couldn't keep that job for very long. The hours made it difficult to work on the business. They needed me five days a week, during the day. Most of my advertising clients worked 9am-5pm, Monday to Friday. I drove the food truck for six weeks while searching for another evening waitressing job. I wasn't actually looking specifically for a golf course, but of course, that was the opportunity that found me.

The third golf course I ended up working at was where I learned that people with money can get away with anything—shocking, I know.

It was a private golf course, and their members paid a significant amount in monthly fees and yearly dues for the luxury of golfing on their lush greens and dining in their upscale lounge. These private members had many special privileges.

There are laws in Canada about over-serving alcohol to patrons, as there should be. There are also serious laws about drinking and driving. None of these laws applied to the patrons at the private course, and we were told to look the other way if a member was intoxicated or out of control. I personally would insist that my manager was the one to continue serving them once I knew they were well over the limit. I didn't want to be liable, legally or morally, if something tragic happened.

I was newly single and trying desperately to balance our new business, waitressing, and my part-time job in the cafeteria. I kept myself as busy as possible, because my personal life was falling apart. The turmoil in my life outside of work, combined with my hectic schedule developed into hyperthyroidism. It runs in my family and is typically brought out by stress.

I was suddenly sick and needed to slow down. Unfortunately, I still needed money, so I made the tough decision to slow down on the business. I was having a hard time acting professional and interacting with business owners because my confidence had been crushed. The waitressing and cafeteria positions required less brain power. The business was still struggle to make a profit and neglecting it was only making it worse.

Roadblocks and Detours

After two years of trying to make it a success, I finally gave up on my dream. I was now in a serious relationship with my soon-to-be husband, William, and the crazy schedule made it challenging to spend any time together. He had four children, and I was missing out on family time. I didn't grow up in a close-knit family, but I wanted to be an active part of this one. My new love gave me an instant family, which meant my priorities needed to change.

I'd open the business as a newly single and highly ambitious woman, and threw in the towel because it interfered with me being a stepmom and a wife. This goes against my current feminist belief system, since I now believe in making your own goals your first priority. I think most women sacrifice too much for their men and their children. Women need to make sure that their own needs are met, as well. However, these were new and delicate relationships that truly mattered to me. The relationships needed nurturing if they were to survive, and I don't regret my decision.

I started looking for office work, and was fortunate to find a fantastic position in the marketing field. I landed a marketing specialist position at a concrete company. The industry was very new to me, but I had an understanding and helpful manager who did an excellent job of teaching me about their scope of work.

This job instantly felt like it could be my dream job. It was a creative position where I could utilize my advertising and marketing background. I was in charge of designing various promotional pieces for the company. I had my own office, with a door, and a relaxed manager who encouraged me to work independently. I truly lucked out.

Unfortunately, my dream job wouldn't last very long at all.

It was the shortest job in my professional career history and has never made it onto my resume. The worst part about this failure was that I had no one to blame it on, other than myself. I destroyed an awesome job that fit perfectly within my fifteen year plan.

I immediately impressed my manager and the owner with my creative designs and my innovative marketing ideas, so my talents weren't to blame. I once flooded the ladies washroom and was too embarrassed to tell anyone, but even that humiliating faux-pas was not responsible for my short-lived stint in the world of concrete marketing.

My emotions got the better of me. It didn't take long for me to become annoyed with the chauvinistic owner. He treated his assistant like a 1950s housewife, and made ridiculous demands just to make himself feel more important. It was nauseating, and I was just starting to notice how women are treated differently in the workplace.

The owner of the company assigned me several tasks that had nothing to do with marketing the concrete business, like preparing things for his wife's birthday and ordering memorial plaques in honor of his parents. It was the plaques that led to my sudden unemployment. As requested, I sent the owner, Antonio Russo, an email outlining the costs for the plaque.

Mr. Russo,
The total cost for the plaques is $550. Each plaque is $150, plus $50/plaque for the engraving, and $75/plaque for the gold-leave embossing. Please let me know if you would like me to proceed.
Thank you,
Jenn

About an hour later, Mr. Russo stopped in my office to discuss the email.

"Where did you get $550 from those costs you sent me?"

"That's the total for both plaques."

"I know women are usually not very good at math, but you better double check your numbers before you send them to me. I looked at it and the math works out to $425."

"I must have mistyped it, let me check."

I opened up the email in a panic that I didn't send him the right costs. I double-checked it against the quote (which was attached to the email) before I hit send, so I couldn't understand how a mistake like that had gotten past me. I was relieved when I opened the email and it matched the quote.

"It says $150 for each plaque, which is $300, plus $50 per plaque for the engraving and $75 each for the embossing. That's $550."

"Your email didn't say $50 and $75 per plaque. You need to be clearer when you send me estimates."

"Sorry, Mr. Russo."

I looked back at the email and it clearly stated $50/plaque. Maybe he didn't understand the / symbol represented per? I've used it in so many past jobs that I couldn't imagine he didn't recognize the meaning I had intended. He was a successful business man.

Rationalizing his rude behavior didn't last very long; soon my confusion turned into frustration and rage at his demeaning insult. Women are usually not very good at math? Math is not my strong suit, but I can do basic math in my head and I'm careful with a calculator. I didn't make a mistake and I needed to vent. So, I decide to send the email to my friend Rachel and get her opinion on what happened. Of course, I added my own commentary before I hit send.

Rachel,

Read the email below and tell me if my math is right. This ego-testical, short Italian prick of a man said my math was wrong and that even though "women are not very good at math," I should have double-checked my numbers before I sent them to him. Fucking loser doesn't know that / means per? He thought the total was $425. Is my math right?

I fired off the fiery email in a about a minute and hit send without giving it a second thought. I needed my friend to back my opinion and validate my anger. A notification immediately appeared on my screen that made me want to melt into the floor.

Your email has been sent to Antonio Russo.

What?

Oh no, what did I just do?

My heart instantly started to race. I double-checked my sent folder and I hit reply instead of forward. I accidentally clicked on his reply to my original email, which I didn't even realize he had sent. The email I selected when I went to forward it to Rachel was Mr. Russo's reply. He must have sent it just prior to stopping in my office.

All it said was, *please correct your math and resend this for my review.*

My heart was beating so rapidly that I wanted to throw up. I just sent the owner of the company an email calling him a short, ego-testical prick and a loser. I knew he had a temper, and I could only imagine his reaction while he read my scathing email.

I didn't know what to do, so I hid in the women's washroom. It was the only place I knew he couldn't find me. There was still an hour left of work and I wasn't ready to confront my horrendous mistake.

Lucky for me, I was able to slip out at 5 o'clock without running into Mr. Russo. I couldn't imagine ever looking him in the face again. Obviously, escaping work that day unseen didn't mean my job was still secure. I drove home knowing that my career with the concrete company was over.

I choked back tears the entire way home and then burst into them as I retold the story to my future husband, William. There was no doubt in my mind that I would be fired the next day. I spent the evening calling my mother and every friend I had to retell the story of my stupidity.

As I mentioned earlier, that story has actually been repeated beyond my inner circle and I've been introduced more than once as the person who hit reply instead of send, and called her boss an ego-testical, short, Italian prick. My emotionally-charged mistake is now a fable or old wives' tale that teaches other hotheaded employees to be more careful before clicking on the send button.

It was never meant to embarrass me—nor did it—since I saw the humor in it once I had secured a new job. It was a mistake, and it doesn't make me a bad employee or a bad person.

Although, at the time in my life when it happened, I felt like a horrible person who would never land another decent job. I sent out about a dozen resumes that night to every job even remotely in my field. I left the job at the concrete company off of my resume. I was certain I had permanently ruined that valuable reference.

Surprisingly, I still managed the courage to show up at work the next day. I tried to pretend nothing happened. I emailed out the company newsletter and responded to a few emails. After almost an hour of sweating and shaking, wondering how and when the bomb would drop, my kind manager asked me into his office. We rarely met in his office, so I braced myself for the inevitable.

"I heard about an email you sent yesterday."

I nodded sheepishly.

"You know that you can't keep your job here."

I nodded again. I didn't want to speak, out of fear that I would cry. It was my first time being fired and I knew I deserved it. I was petrified this brutal mistake would stick with me and make it difficult to find future employment.

My manager walked me back to my office, watched me pack up my stuff, and escorted me out of the building. I immediately broke down in tears the moment I got inside my car. I couldn't pull out of the parking lot until I was able to catch my breath. Both my parents have a strong work ethic, and my mother always stressed the importance of being a loyal and respectful employee. My dad made me paranoid that one mistake in the workplace could ruin my entire career. When it happened that day, I thought I had ruined my entire life.

Fortunately for me, I was wrong.

A Big Step Backwards

I was lucky enough to land on my feet and found a new job willing to hire me after only a few days of searching. Unfortunately, I took the first job I was offered, because I was afraid that there wouldn't be any other offers. It was a secretarial/shipping clerk position at a hardware distributor. It was a massive step in the wrong direction, as well as a pay cut, but I had too much debt to be without an income for very long.

The role came with two desks and it turned out to be more challenging than I initially thought. I was responsible for all of the secretarial, purchasing, shipping, and receiving duties. I started my day by preparing the paperwork for all the outgoing customer shipments in the receiving office, and then switched to the front desk to deliver any intercompany mail, enter any supplier invoices, and order any necessary supplies. I appreciated the fact that it kept me busy and the days went by fast. Throughout my career, I've always preferred to be busy at work. Working at the hardware distribution company kept me plenty busy.

However, it had more interoffice politics and rumors than my previous employment experience. It became pretty obvious early on that the general manager had an exceptionally close relationship with his assistant, Tanya. She was able to get away with doing hardly anything, she felt comfortable talking down to more senior employees despite being only an assistant, and she spent a suspicious amount of time in his office with the door shut. I have no real evidence to suggest they were having an affair, but it was the common opinion throughout the office. Several other employees saw them out together in public. I could only speculate.

I didn't trust the general manager for reasons beyond his fondness for a much younger assistant. Although his almost-undeniable infidelity bothered me because he was only recently married, and it was to a lovely woman whom I had met on several occasions, that wasn't the problem that made me lose respect for him as a manager. I didn't trust his business ethics.

Our office was the Canadian branch of a company located in the United States. The general manager was in charge of the Canadian branch and ran it somewhat independently. The American headquarters, however, managed the books for our location. Headquarters didn't visit our facility, at least not while I worked there, so my boss would sometimes put through questionable invoices that didn't arrive in the regular company mail.

For example, he put through an invoice for a new roof and I was quite certain it wasn't for our office or warehouse. If the building needed work on the roof, he would have asked me to request quotes. I never saw any roofing vehicles on the property during working hours. Plus, I knew the general manager was in the process of restoring an older home for himself and his new bride.

I have a hard time hiding my disapproval towards people who get away with bad behavior. I feel like I've been burned for every bad decision I've made, and my follies never go unnoticed. It bothered me that the general manager was so ethically corrupt, yet he had a beautiful wife, a great job, brand new car, and was in the process of building his dream house.

Where's the justice?

However, every job has pros and cons. I was good at my job, and was given a promotion after only six months with the company. They hired a recent graduate to fill my previous position and moved me into a role that better suited my abilities; sales and marketing. I worked with clients to place their orders and answer any of their concerns. It was an interesting job, but the unavoidable drama didn't allow it to last very long.

The general manager's assistant wanted the sales job, and despite her connection with the only decision-maker in the office, I was chosen over her. My promotion put a sizeable target on my back. Tanya didn't like the attention I was suddenly getting from the general manager, and began to cause problems for everyone at work.

Her superior attitude kicked into overdrive; she was determined to flaunt her power. After a closed-door meeting with the general manager, Tanya was given her own corner office and a title change, human resources coordinator. The general manager had taken care of all the HR related duties up until this point and it was frightening discovering that it would now be in her hands. Even worse, her new office made her feel even more important. Therefore, the unbearable nitpicking and work-dumping increased.

Tanya wasn't the only reason I knew I wouldn't be retiring from the hardware distributor. Another obvious imbalance I couldn't accept was the pay difference between the men and women in my department. There were five internal employees who handled sales. The only other female had the most seniority, but confided in me that she only made $18.00 per hour, which she knew was $4.00 less per hour than her male counterparts.

I couldn't fathom such blatant inequality and mistreatment of women, so I asked one of the new guys what he felt I should be making in my new role and he said, "I would assume pretty close to what I make, $22.00 per hour." He was still relatively new himself, and it confirmed her suspicions were true. I was making only $14.00 per hour. I was new, but knowing this kind, hard-working woman with eighteen years seniority was making $4.00 less than a young guy with little experience who had only been with the company two years, didn't make sense to me.

Thankfully, a better opportunity found me. A local department store saw my resume posted online and asked me to come in for an interview. I had posted it on the site when my poor judgment cost me the great job at the concrete company. The store had an excellent reputation throughout the city, as far as I knew, and the role itself sounded perfect for me.

I felt confident the job would be mine after the first interview, so I did something boldly out-of-character; I gave my two weeks' notice at the hardware distributor before being hired. I was dreading going to work each day because of the drama, and felt certain this was my way out. I was beginning to trust that a new door would always open, if I had the guts to close the one I was currently standing in. Fortunately, my instincts were right.

I made a commitment to myself when I landed the job at the large, family-owned department store. I was tired of starting over and I promised myself that I would do everything I could to retire from the next place I worked. I was done chasing my fifteen year plan; I wanted job security. I would be a model employee, put in the extra effort required, and develop a strong relationship with my next boss. I was not going to allow my foolishness or the poor behavior of other people push me out of another job.

My new boss was Baumann's Director of Marketing and Purchasing, Agnes Jones. Most importantly to me, my new boss was a woman. It was the first time I'd had a female boss, outside of the hospitality industry. It was reassuring to see a woman with so much power and influence in a professional environment. I could tell she was tough, and I felt certain she was the example I needed to achieve the success I've always desired.

I could instantly tell that Agnes Jones commanded respect; or at least what I assumed to be respect, at that time. I now realize I was misinterpreting fear and loathing as admiration. It was an impressionable time in my life and I was looking for a strong female role model. I thought Agnes would make the perfect boss for the next and final chapter in my career.

Agnes wasn't particular fussy about her appearance. She had dark auburn hair with noticeable grey streaks and dark rimmed, outdated eyeglasses. She mainly wore tapered, bland business suits and short, sensible heels with her hair tied back in a neat bun. She wasn't physically fit or abnormally overweight. I figured it was pretty safe to assume she wasn't sexually appealing enough to have gotten by on her looks alone, so it must have been her strong business sense and hard work ethic that were responsible for her rise to the top.

That was the example I wanted to follow! I was eager and ambitious right from the beginning. Once again, I took extensive notes and tried to absorb everything my experienced and successful new boss had to teach me. There was so much to learn, and I was ecstatic to finally have a tough female role model in my life.

By the end of the first month, I had mapped out my expected rise from marketing assistant to director of marketing and purchasing. I calculated that I would be ready for the responsibility just in time for Agnes to retire; approximately fifteen years from when I was first hired. I was back on track in regards to my preparation and experience first methodology, but I had a new goal in my sights.

In reality, I was the newest person at the department store and there was already a long line of qualified candidates striving to one day fill her shoes. She was basically at the top of the company (aside from various family members), and I'd just started there in an entry-level position. I still had a very long way to go.

I was grateful to discover that the job itself was pretty interesting, as well. The department store carried clothing, cosmetics, toys, small appliances, electronics, home furnishings, and various accessories. It was my responsibility to ensure we always had stock of any houseware and home furnishing items. Determining the demand could be simplified to a basic formula, if it was consistent. Anyone who's ever worked retail knows sales can fluctuate drastically without warning or reason.

I had to monitor the trends and place enough on order to make sure we always had stock for instant delivery, if it was a sale or regular stock item. I also handled custom orders for a few of the designer sofa sets and recliners we carried. I had to make sure that the customer's specific requirements were clearly and accurately communicated to the vendor.

I managed the stock for hundreds of different SKUs and dealt with anywhere from twenty to thirty different suppliers at a time. I had to be organized, detail-oriented, and flexible with my priorities. I also needed a thick skin.

Agnes was direct and curt with her instructions. She rarely complimented anything I did, nor did she thank me for going above and beyond on requests she gave me. I was trying my best to impress her, but I wasn't receiving the response I'd anticipated. I was used to bosses praising me because I always did more than I should in an attempt to win them over. I couldn't win over Agnes, despite my greatest efforts.

Baumann's Department Store, however, won me over almost immediately. I started working at the department store a couple months before Thanksgiving and one of my first and favorite memories of working there was their annual appreciation celebration. It gave me a warm feeling of family and job security that stuck with me until I was forced out, nearly five years later.

Everyone gathered in one of the large showrooms for the traditional toast from the company's president. There was coffee, donuts, muffins and genuine cheer throughout the room. The year I started was the same year that the previous owner had retired and passed the business on to his son, Sean Baumann.

The new president seemed humble and sincerely grateful for everyone's contributions to the success of his family's business. He was a handsome young man, ready to leap into his father's shoes with determination and enthusiasm. In all honesty, he didn't look old enough to handle the massive challenge. He had boyish blonde hair, light blue eyes, and a soft baby face. I guessed we were pretty close in age and I knew I wasn't quite ready for that level of responsibility. I couldn't manage a two person advertising agency.

The celebration began with Sean Baumann telling everyone the story of how the business began with his grandfather, had been passed onto his father, and how proud he was to be following in their footsteps. He was a passionate and confident speaker who sincerely inspired me. It truly made me feel like this could be the place where I retire.

They announced the names of any employees who had been with the company longer than ten years. The store was filled with long-term staff members who must have been kept happy enough to stay. There were even people who had been with the store for twenty and thirty years. Discovering this history of longevity and family-oriented traditions gave me reassurance, since I can't accurately express just how tired I was of bouncing from one business to the next. My resume was starting to resemble a novel.

Oddly enough, I would later turn my resume into a novel.

At the end of the event, the company gave every employee a ham and a Thanksgiving bonus; store gift certificates. It was a very generous gesture, considering the company also owned a second department store in Leamington, which employed another eighty people on top of the two hundred working at the Windsor location.

I finally had a job at an appreciative company, with an intelligent female boss, and the work itself was interesting. I decorated my desk with family photos, made some wonderful new friends, and embraced my new career path fully. I felt like I was finally home.

The first two years I worked there went pretty smoothly and it was the happiest I'd ever been with a job. I enjoyed the work I did, and I got along with pretty much everyone in the company. There was mild work drama, as there is everywhere, but nothing that would interfere with my new fifteen year plan.

I noticed there was exceptionally high turnover in the Marketing and Purchasing department and other people in the company repeatedly warned me about Agnes' temper and disrespectful behavior, but I hadn't really seen it firsthand. I saw a mentor who was trying to toughen me up, so I could be a better buyer.

Agnes gave me great reviews, and worked with me one on one to improve my weak areas. Her greatest criticism of me was that I was a people pleaser. She disapproved of how I catered to the sales staff. She was right; it was true. I may have argued it back then, but I can admit now that I was wrong. My self-esteem was still shaky and I needed people to like me. However, I also felt the sales staff deserved my attention.

Agnes didn't care who liked her.

She seemed to delight in ruffling people's feathers and didn't care if some of her decisions had a negative effect on other employees. I was often the one responsible for implementing and enforcing her unfavorable ideas. It didn't matter if I disagreed with her decisions. I was always voicing my opinion to deaf ears, so I eventually stopped.

Agnes wanted me to spend less time helping the sales staff, and our Customer Care Department, so I could take on more work. I felt they were key to the company's success. These people were the gateway to our customers, and a happy customer is a repeat customer. I ended up taking on the additional work and discreetly assisting our sales and customer care teams when Agnes wasn't in earshot.

After I was at the department store for two years, Agnes made the decision to hire a merchandise manager to oversee the three marketing assistants and our merchandising coordinator. She needed to free up more of her time for higher-level tasks.

The three assistants and merchandising coordinator, as well as a few other internal employees, were given the first opportunity to apply for the position. I desperately wanted the position, but assumed that Maria, the marketing assistant who handled the entertainment and electronic division, had the best chance. She had the most seniority in our department.

I spent the next two days using my free time to prep for the interview. I wanted to know the entire department store`s layout, inventory cycles, and top selling product SKUs by heart. The store carried everything from clothing and cosmetics to houseware and furniture. There was a lot to cram into my brain, although the details for the categories I was currently responsible for were already there. I knew my own SKUs inside and out.

The interview went well, but I got the sense that I wasn't being taken very seriously. It was probably pre-determined that Maria would receive the promotion, since she had a long and positive history with the company—as far as I knew. The interview felt like it was more of a formality that had no real bearing on the outcome.

I was right about not being a serious consideration for the role. However, I was quite surprised to discover that the new manager would be an outside hire. The fact that they decided not to promote from within wasn't a promising start to my slow and steady rise to the top. Maria and Bill, the other marketing assistants, had to rise up the ladder so that I could move up a rung.

The woman they chose for the position seemed nice, but something about her felt artificial. Her smile was tense, her posture stiff, and she didn't really look you in the eye when she spoke to you. She was a few inches taller than me; it always felt like she was talking to my forehead. She had dark brown eyes, and beautiful blonde hair with a slight curl that rested on her shoulders. Unlike Agnes, she wore modern, fitted suits and skirts from top designers with ridiculously high heels. She would have been quite stunning if she'd smiled more often.

She was going to be my new boss, so I was determined to win her over. I still hadn't impressed Agnes and viewed the new merchandising manager, Yvonne Dejardin, as my chance to shine. I planned on using all of my experience and research to help Yvonne adjust to her new role. I gave her the notes I prepared for the interview, ran reports I thought she would find useful, and jumped at any of her requests for assistance. As Agnes had stated, I was a people pleaser and I went above and beyond to please my managers.

Yes, you could call me a brownnoser. There is too much evidence for me to deny it.

Yvonne and I started off on the right foot, despite the fact that she always spoke down to me. I don't have much of an ego and it never bothered me. She barked orders, never admitted her mistakes, and demanded more from me than she was willing to do herself. She was a typical boss, just like Agnes. I was used to it, and I could handle it.

Baumann's art director, who also worked under Agnes, quit about a year after Yvonne was hired. The art director was responsible for developing and creating all of the advertising for both store locations. It was very similar to the role I'd had in my own business. It was also a chance for me to redirect my career, back into real marketing and copywriting. The thought of it reignited a creative fire inside of me.

I hadn't written anything in an over a year and I missed it. I was confident I could write compelling ad copy for Baumann's, and spent the next few days developing a variety of different campaigns. This would be the perfect opportunity to impress Agnes. I was determined not to waste it.

Still Far Off Course

U nfortunately that interview didn't go as I'd planned, either. My advertising ideas weren't reviewed at all, and I was rushed out as being unqualified. Agnes told me afterwards that they couldn't hire me for it because I didn't have any management experience, and the job would involve managing our graphic design team. She was polite, but completely dismissive when I suggested that I was confident I would make a good leader.

Of course I felt discouraged, but the current art director advised me that her decision was for the best. He warned me that directors at Baumann's had to be cutthroat. He said it was a demanding and thankless position where your ideas are never taken into consideration.

Despite the fact that I didn't get the art director position, everything was going relatively well at work until I received my first review from Yvonne. I'd received high marks on the three previous reviews given by Agnes, so I was shocked to see average and below average scores from Yvonne. The worst was a below par score on my communication skills. Communication skills were my strongest category on previous reviews. I always kept the company and Yvonne informed of what was going on, and I responded to any correspondence quickly and professionally.

However, that wasn't what the review said. The review even mentioned specific incidents where I hadn't informed Yvonne of delays or problems in a timely manner. I immediately recognized that I had written proof I did indeed inform her of at least two situations she had listed on the review. When I mentioned to Yvonne that I had proof, she argued and then crossed those notes off the review, without changing my score.

There were also low scores on the review for innovation and dedication. Six months earlier I won an internal customer service award for my passion, voted on by the department store staff. Surely that should prove I was a dedicated employee. I came up with many creative and unique ideas, advertising campaigns, and merchandising strategies since I started there, and almost all were completely ignored.

I explained this to Yvonne, and she dismissed me coldly.

"You don't work nearly enough overtime, and you haven't given us any valuable or innovative ideas. In my opinion, you need development in both of those categories, as well as your communication skills. I am putting you on 90-day probation until I see more initiative out of you."

"Probation?"

My eyes widened and my jaw dropped. I was in complete disbelief. I was a hard-working and respected employee who rarely made mistakes. In fact, I spent a lot of time finding and correcting Yvonne's mistakes. I knew in my heart that I didn't deserve to be put on probation, and I didn't understand what I had done to earn such a negative review. I tried to get a better explanation of the real reason for the bad review, since nothing she was saying made any sense to me. I'm not trying to be arrogant; I just know I was a hard-working employee and the review was not fair.

However, as a survivor of an abusive personal relationship and a chronic self-conscience worrywart, I can easily be convinced that I'm worthless. My self-doubt consumes me at times, and she had me in tears by the time I left our closed-door meeting. I started to question everything I did and my own capabilities.

I went home and told my husband, mother, and best friend about the review. All three insisted that I speak to our human resources department. Yvonne was fairly new, and had already made a few costly mistakes against my better advice. One of those mistakes was listed in the review as my error. I had an email proving otherwise. I repeatedly warned her verbally and in writing that an item wouldn't arrive in time for a sale, prior to the sales flyers being prepared. When it didn't arrive in time for a sale, it appeared she had blamed me.

I felt certain I must be her fall guy to Agnes.

I asked a few co-workers who knew me and my work ethic. None of them were fans of Yvonne, since I wasn't the only person that she treated with disrespect. They agreed with my family and friends. Yvonne was most likely making me look like the one who faltered to avoid the wrath of Agnes. So, I made an appointment with our human resources manager.

I showed the HR expert my past reviews, my current reviews, and the evidence I had to dispute Yvonne's negative comments on the review. The HR manager knew I was a good employee. Even though we never worked directly together, she was the one who read all of the nomination other employees submitted when I won the internal customer service award. She had told me a few months prior that I'd received twice as many votes as anyone else. When I showed her my evidence, she agreed that the grading and comments did not add up and they could not possibly be a true testament of my performance.

Any human resources professional will tell you that an employee's review should never come as a complete shock. Coaching and constructive commentary should be given throughout the year by the manager, so the employee is aware when there is a problem with their performance. This was the first I was hearing that my communication, innovation, and dedication were in question. That by itself was a red flag that something suspicious was going on.

She advised me to talk to Agnes directly and resolve this obvious injustice. I must admit that I was nervous approaching Agnes. We hadn't worked closer together since Yvonne started, and she never really seemed like she was all that fond of me.

However, I was confident that she couldn't ignore the physical evidence. She knew I was good at my job, and had given me a high grade on my communication skills in past reviews. It was time for me to stand my ground and defend what I knew was right. I took a deep breath and made an appointment to meet with Agnes the following morning.

That meeting was my first glimpse into the real Agnes. She didn't give me a chance to talk and had no interest in looking at the examples I brought with me. She backed up Yvonne's assessment of me and tried to twist it into something different. She implied that I resented Yvonne for getting that position and that I was now being insubordinate by questioning my performance review. She reinforced Yvonne's negative assessment of my work ethic and dedication.

I was sincerely shocked by her accusations, but not nearly as shocked as I was later that day. Yvonne found out that I went to Agnes with my review, probably from Agnes, and called me in for another unpleasant meeting.

"I can't believe you went to Agnes. Whose idea did you think it was to give you that review?"

My jaw dropped opened in disbelief. I guess I'm pretty naïve, because it never occurred to me that Agnes would have been responsible for my first bad review. About 90 percent of my job was dealing directly with Yvonne. Agnes was a busy woman and usually dealing with higher-level issues. She wouldn't have any idea about my performance unless it came from Yvonne.

I went back to HR to discuss what had just happened and she told me that Agnes explained my review to her and she completely altered her opinion about it. I couldn't believe how quickly her mind had been changed. I'm pretty sure she just wasn't willing to stick her neck out and go up against Agnes. I now understand the kind of damage Agnes can cause when you get on her bad side, and I no longer blame the HR manager for letting me down.

However, I couldn't understand why they would want to deliberately sabotage me. I knew I was an asset to the department store and had treated both of them with respect. It was obvious that I cared a lot about Baumann's and my co-workers. I felt completely blindsided by what happened and it took me years before I was able to make any sense out of it.

After Yvonne scolded me for disputing my review and taking it to Agnes, she then proceeded to outline how she was going to conduct and evaluate my probation period. I was asked to meet with her once a week to discuss my progress. I would also need to demonstrate improvement in the three areas where I was "lacking" by the end of the three-month period.

Yvonne, under the guidance of Agnes, would determine if I was successful. They would be the sole judges who would assess if I had proven dedication, innovation, and strong communication skills.

I could not stop crying that night. My family and friends couldn't comfort me despite their best efforts. The two people who would ultimately decide if I get to keep a job I loved more than any previous position just gave me an undeserved poor review and put me on probation.

I was screwed.

I needed to expose the truth and find a way to save my job, before it was too late. My first idea was to catch Yvonne on tape, so no one could deny the evidence. I borrowed a friend's tape recorder and brought it into my next closed door meeting with Yvonne. I calmly listened as she attacked my work ethic and company loyalty, while outlining her agenda and expectations for the week. I eagerly agreed to do everything she asked, so they could say I was being difficult. For the record, I always did anything she asked of me without attitude or dispute. Those who know me will believe that statement without any hesitation. I'm an agreeable employee in general.

The conversation I attempted to record wasn't hard evidence of the bullying and lies, but it was a good start. Unfortunately, our voices sounded like the adults in a Charlie Brown cartoon. I tested it afterwards and you had to talk directly into the recorder in order for it to pick up anything comprehensible.

I was determined to obtain some evidence that I was still an asset to the company and that the real mistakes were trickling down from above, so I bought an expensive tape recorder and kept the receipt so I could return it after I got my evidence (it was significantly beyond my budget, especially when I was in fear of losing my job). I placed it in my suit jacket pocket and went into my second follow-up meeting.

Yvonne tried to imply that I wasn't meeting her expectations, but I gave her specific examples where I did and she couldn't come up with any accurate ones where I didn't. I kept detailed records of all our conversations and any email evidence in which she acknowledged my strong communication skills. I brought it with me to the meeting and countered each of her comments with the truth.

"I told you yesterday morning about that issue as soon as you came in. Remember, you told me you would come up with a substitution, and then I emailed you a few possible replacements a couple hours later."

"Oh yes, that's right. I guess you are improving."

This time, the tape recorder only caught my end of our conversation. Her voice was too faint to understand. So, I tried again the following week with the tape recorder stuck up the sleeve of my jacket. I got as close to the desk as I possibly could, but it still wasn't a usable recording. I finally realized that I had to stop trying to catch her bad behavior and focus solely on keeping my job.

I might have had an easier time later on at Baumann's if I had just been squeezed out of the department store after the 90-day probation. I should have known the happiness and job security I felt prior to the bad review would never exist again.

A Rocky Uphill Climb

I loved my job for the first four years. I've also never been a too-proud-to-beg kind of person, so I sucked it up, kissed their asses, and went above and beyond to prove my worthiness. I actually spread that new resilient passion outside of the workplace and decided to challenge myself to be a more confident and capable person in all aspects of my life.

At that time in my life, I was an overweight smoker. I had a good marriage, but I was insecure, especially when it came to my body. I was also a typical woman, which meant I would run myself ragged caring for my husband and my step-kids, while rarely doing anything for myself.

I wasn't unhappy, but at the same time, I wasn't really making the most out of my life. Maybe Agnes and Yvonne had some valid points. Maybe my drive and determination needed an overhaul. I used to be so ambitious; maybe being turned down for multiple positions was chipping away at my hope and motivation. I needed to set goals and aim higher.

One of my close friends from the department store ran her first marathon earlier that year and brought her medal to work. The medal was impressive, but it was her genuine pride in herself that I found contagious and inspiring. She worked hard and accomplished something incredibly difficult. She earned that sense of achievement.

I wanted that same feeling of pride.

I had high self-esteem until my mid-teens, but it spiraled out of control in my early twenties. I became a doormat and a doer, not a leader. It was an easy and comfortable role that I accepted without question. Sadly, when I'm insecure and meek, I'm also easy to ignore.

I wasn't meant to be ignored. I have too many powerful messages that I insist on sharing. I know now my life was never meant to be easy and comfortable. I've discovered that I'm capable of creating positive change. I recalled people listening to me when I was young and secure in myself. That confidence and courage still existed inside of me; I just needed to revive it.

The sudden setback in my career fueled my new perspective, and I decided that I was done discounting myself. I immediately set two personal goals that I knew would build my confidence back up, because they both seemed daunting and impossible at the time. I was going to finish a half-marathon and quit smoking.

It was early March. I decided I would quit smoking on my thirtieth birthday in June, and then attempt to run the Detroit International half-marathon in October. The dates were realistic and I felt very motivated. Most people who knew me at that time found it doubtful, which only made me more determined to be successful. Some even told me I wouldn't do it. My brother was one of them, but only because he knew that was the exact motivation I would need to cross the finish line. I wouldn't quit until I proved him wrong.

I'm proud to admit that I not only accomplished those goals, but I also finished a full marathon the following year. I'm not a fast runner, and I usually need to walk for a few minutes of every mile, but I've successfully completed five half-marathons and two full-marathons since I set that goal, six years ago. I'm living proof that anyone can change their life.

Even better, I'm proof that miracles do happen. At the end of my probation, I ended up meeting all of the requirements outlined three months earlier by Yvonne. She even rewarded me with a luxurious gift that she picked up for me while she was on vacation. I was starting to realize that Yvonne was simply Agnes's minion, not her accomplice.

My efforts to work my way back into their good graces paid off initially, but sadly, it didn't last very long. A few months later, Agnes decided the department needed to mix up the roles to create more defined positions.

Instead of each marketing assistant being responsible for all the re-ordering, merchandising, and trend analysis for their specific area of the store, there would be two clerks responsible for the data entry aspect of the job, and two senior positions that would handle the more creative and analytical tasks; determining store layout, sales strategies, and trend analysis. The four people working under Agnes and Yvonne would either become a sales & marketing specialist or a purchasing coordinator.

I didn't want to be a coordinator. It would be strictly administrative duties. The data entry aspect of the position I already handled was very monotonous. I knew that would become my entire job if I ended up in that role, and it would make me miserable within a year. I viewed it as a step backwards in my career, and thought I was the only one on the team who had any marketing and sales experience prior to Baumann's. I knew the sales & marketing specialist position was the right one for me, and I was determined to convince my inconvincible boss as well.

I went in to work on the weekend—unpaid—and prepared a six-page presentation of explaining our current sales trends, as well as potential marketing strategies for boosting sales. I bought slick black folders and made a copy for each person who would be attending the internal interview. I was ready to wow them with my professionalism and knowledge.

As far as I know, I'm the only one who went the extra mile to prove their worthiness. I didn't share my strategy with my co-workers so I would have the advantage. I desperately wanted the position of sales & marketing specialist versus the purchasing coordinator role and I truly believed I had what it took to land it. Yes, I'm an unrealistic dreamer, considering I was just coming off of probation.

Unfortunately, the interview didn't go as I'd planned. Once again, I felt like they were not interested in my ideas and the questions were intended to bring out my weaknesses. The interview consisted of Agnes, the men's apparel buyer, and the human resources manager. I stayed calm and professional no matter what they asked me, and thought I had at least impressed the HR manager.

However, I was offered the purchasing coordinator position two days later. Yvonne told me that my strong organizational and administrative

skills made me the ideal candidate. I couldn't disguise the look of disappointment in my face when she broke the news to me. She looked sad, as
well. We had been getting along surprisingly well for the past few months,
and she knew how much I wanted to be one of the sales & marketing spe-
cialists. I told her I was disappointed with the decision, because I thought
I did well in the interview. Yvonne was very comforting.

"I heard you did great. Agnes said you sold yourself really well, and
she was impressed by the work you put into it. However, you know once
Agnes makes her mind up about someone, there is no changing it. This is
the role she wants you in."

I burst into tears as soon as she said it. It was the second time I had
cried in front of Yvonne and this time she was kind enough to offer me
Kleenex to wipe my face. She hadn't done that when I cried during my
unfair review eight months earlier. I could tell she was sincerely sympathetic. I had been with the company for over four years, and my first move
would be backwards. I was devastated.

I had booked off the following day for my annual doctor and dentist
appointments, so I asked if I could take a day to think about the offer. I
wasn't ready to enthusiastically sign up for a data- entry coordinator position. She agreed to give me a day or two to think about it, and then suggested there might be other roles in the company that might better suit my
skills.

"You sold yourself well in the interview and our sales staff makes really
good money. Have you ever considered applying for sales?"

"I used to sell magazine ad space and was quite successful. Do you
think the company would let me switch to sales?"

"Why not? You're well liked, you know the products inside and out,
and you've got that chipper personality that's perfect for sales. Talk to Paul,
and see what he thinks. If you don't want the coordinator position, I'm
sure we can find something more suitable. It's a big company."

I thanked her for the suggestion and raced to see the sales manager.
Paul was a friend of mine and thrilled with the idea. He told me he would
love to have me on his staff, as long as Agnes and Yvonne agreed. I told
him that it was Yvonne's idea and I'm sure the three of us could convince

Agnes. I left that day feeling great, despite receiving the disappointing news about the sales and marketing specialist position.

I enjoyed the next day of appointments and running errands, because I felt confident I would still be a Baumann's employee. I wasn't ready to give up on the years I had invested in the company, and I had no desire to start somewhere new. I also decided I would take the coordinator position if Agnes didn't want me in the sales role. Baumann's was my family, and I didn't want to work for any other company.

As soon as I came into work the next day, there was a request from the sales manager to set up an official interview with him for later that morning, and a meeting request from Yvonne. She specifically said that she wanted to discuss the purchasing coordinator position before my sales interview. Something in my gut told me things had changed drastically while I was enjoying my hectic vacation day. My fears were confirmed as soon as I entered Yvonne's office.

"I could tell you were not sincerely interested in the purchasing coordinator position, so we are taking back our offer. If you were truly willing to do it, you would have signed the new contract when it was offered to you on Tuesday"

Her voice was flat and deflated.

"What?"

"You didn't sign the offer when it was presented, and chose to look for another job at the company. We need someone who will embrace the role with enthusiasm, and that is obviously not you."

I begged and pleaded with her to reconsider, but she wouldn't look me in the eyes. My husband was in a retraining program at the local college and I couldn't afford to lose my job. I knew the jobs in Windsor were scarce, and I was no longer the big risk-taker I had been when I started an ad agency at the age of twenty-three. We depended on my income to survive, and it was never my intent to quit my job. I wouldn't have asked for more time if I thought the job offer would be rescinded.

"You know I would give that role 110 percent if I accepted it, regardless of if I wasn't thrilled about it. It was your idea for me to look into a sales position. I can't afford to be without a job."

"I'm sorry, but I can't give you this offer now and I need your formal resignation."

I was stunned. I was shaking. I couldn't catch my breath or collect my thoughts.

What just happened?

"I don't want to quit."

"Well, your current job ends January 28th, and I can't offer you the sales & marketing specialist position or the purchasing coordinator position. So, you don't really have an option."

My brain was scrambling for a way to talk myself out of it. I would beg, grovel on my hands and knees, anything to keep my job. That store was my second family and I couldn't just leave it. While I sat there in complete shock, Yvonne's words got me thinking. I technically had a job until January 28th. It was December 5th and there was nothing forcing me to resign immediately.

"I need to think about this and look into it before I resign. I still have the sales interview later today, and I'm hoping that works out."

"I need your resignation by tomorrow morning."

I couldn't believe that the job offer was no longer on the table. All I asked for was a day or two to think about it. It was a step back in my career and I wasn't sure if a sales position would be a better fit for me. I never said I was willing to walk away from my career at Baumann's. Yvonne was the one who suggested sales. I doubt that Yvonne had deliberately sent me off in the wrong direction, so I assumed this latest bombshell was being dropped by Agnes. Yvonne was merely one of the queen's puppets, sent out to destroy lives without having to witness the collateral damage.

I didn't cry in front of Yvonne this time, but excused myself and hid in the washroom for ten minutes while I cried. I did my best to calm myself down and return to my desk without drawing any attention. I kept myself from breaking down by convincing myself that I still had a chance of staying with the company.

I was hoping I'd be offered the sales position. If not, maybe I could win over Agnes, prove I was an asset that the company should keep, and get her to change her decision before January 28th. I was still currently employed by the department store and I had a chance to turn this negative into a positive. I did my best to regain my composure and put my mind on winning over the sales manager.

I wouldn't lose my job at Baumann's if I aced the interview, right?

The interview was scheduled for thirty minutes after my meeting with Yvonne. It didn't give me any time to prepare and I was still rattled from the bomb Yvonne just dropped on me. However, I didn't think I would need much preparation.

Paul was an easy-going gentleman who already knew my strong work ethic. I knew the department store's sales strategies and responsibilities almost as well as the current sales staff. I had worked closely with them for nearly five years. Plus, he'd already told me that he would hire me—as long as Agnes and Yvonne agreed. I reassured myself that it would work out for the best, and managed the strength to walk into the interview feeling confident.

Unfortunately, I couldn't have prepared myself for the interview I was about to experience. It was obvious his opinion had changed in one day. I felt like I was on trial. Agnes met with the sales manager prior to the interview, and gave him specific questions to ask. I don't know this for a fact, but I saw him in her office with the door closed; it doesn't make sense that he would come up with those questions on his own. Paul was another puppet.

In the interview, Paul brought up my bad review and how I went to human resources to complain about it and Yvonne. I was shocked that he knew about it, but completely caught off guard by the way he asked me about it.

"It doesn't appear like you can handle constructive criticism."

Paul's tone was different than every conversation we'd had in the last four years, and I could tell something wasn't right. I responded that I learned my weaknesses from the review and had worked hard to improve on them. I also assured him that Yvonne and I had a strong relationship now. I knew from previous conversations that he didn't really care for Agnes or Yvonne, but we both knew how to work with them, regardless of how they treated us.

"Do you want the sales position just so you can get away from Yvonne?"

"I respect Yvonne and it was her idea to apply for sales."

"So, it wasn't your idea to apply for sales."

"Yvonne suggested it. She said I had sold myself well in the sales & marketing specialist interview, but I've been overjoyed about the idea ever since."

"You're jumping at the first opportunity to work for someone else. Are you sure you really want a sales position?"

"I sincerely do. I have worked in sales in the past, and understand the ups and downs of it. I enjoy interacting with people, and I know our sales staff makes good money. I love working at Baumann's, and would be a profitable salesperson for the company."

"Working in sales requires a thick skin. Can you handle it?"

"Of course I can. My current role has me satisfying needs for the sales staff and two demanding bosses. If I can do that with a smile on my face, I'm confident I can care for even the most difficult of customers."

Paul smiled when I said it and then went back to looking somber. I thought I sold myself well, even though it felt more like an interrogation than an interview. I was still worried though, because of the look on his face. His interest from the day before had been completely drained. His eyes looked sympathetic and torn. I had a bad feeling in my gut that this was another formality-inspired interview.

I spent the rest of the afternoon in a daze. I was busy like usual, so I mustered everything inside of me to focus on my work while secretly stressing over the events from the morning. I took a long drive on my lunch break, and debated whether or not I had the courage to go back. However, I wasn't a quitter and I needed my job. I wasn't ready to give up hope.

I finished the day without demonstrating my utter disappointment to anyone. I was too afraid of reprisal if word spread that I confided in anyone about how I was being treated. Agnes ran our department, as well as the company itself. I couldn't go up against her and win. I was pretty sure she made the decision to rescind the job offer and sabotage my interview. Once Agnes made a decision, there was no changing her mind. Yvonne had told me that on numerous occasions.

I knew it was best to keep my feelings to myself until I got home.

At home, I told William, my mom, and Rachel about the latest drama. I started researching employment laws in Ontario, because those who loved me insisted that there must be a law to protect me from being forced out. How could a company make me to resign when I hadn't done anything wrong?

I found a few loopholes that would allow me to collect unemployment and a way that I could still stay with the company for almost another two months, which should give me plenty of time to find a new job.

During my research, I got the "bright" idea to send a compelling email to Agnes, Yvonne, the HR manager, the sales manager, and both of the Baumann sons that would hopefully fix the mess I was in. I've always been better at conveying my intentions on paper than in person.

I wanted to secure my current position for the next two months, hopefully land the sales position, and if not, set myself up for unemployment. I also wanted to show everyone that I was a loyal Baumann employee who didn't want to leave the company. I spent a lot of time choosing my wording to ensure it expressed those precise messages. I emailed myself the message to my work account, so I could send it the following day while I was at work.

Yvonne called me into her office first thing the next morning to inquire on my resignation letter before I got a chance to send the email. She wanted it immediately and said there was no delaying the inevitable. I told her that it was not quite ready and that I needed a little more time. I went back to my desk and sent the email I had prepared.

Good Morning,

First and most importantly, I want to sincerely thank you for recognizing the need for change in our department. We were constantly struggling to stay on top of things, and this new strategy will make it easier on my co-workers. Although I absolutely agree with the changes that were made, regrettably the position of purchasing coordinator is not the direction I want for my career. I request that I maintain my current position until Jan 28, 2011 and hopefully at that time I can relocate within the company. Yvonne had suggested sales when she commented on how well I sold myself in the sales & marketing specialist interview, so hopefully I can still be beneficial to the company in that capacity.

If Baumann's does not find a suitable position for me within the company, please know that I have genuinely loved being part of the Baumann's family. This decision does not come easily for me. The thought of leaving this company has brought me to tears, but it would be a disservice to myself and Baumann's if I accept a position that does not provide me with job satisfaction. I am ready to step up and be challenged in life! Some people felt I should have agreed to the purchasing coordinator position immediately and secretly searched for something better, but I know Baumann's deserves more. If I could not be fully committed to the role, then Yvonne needs time to find a candidate who will be ready to embrace it. As I stated in my interview, I am honest; unfortunately, in life, it does not always work to my advantage.

Yvonne had requested I resign, but I have been advised not to do so. Due to a constructive dismissal law, I may be able to collect unemployment in February. If the company decides I am not right for sales, I need a back-up plan financially. I hope you understand.

Thank you,

Jenn

My email was sincere, and only slightly untrue since I neglected to mention that the job offer was taken away before I made my decision, but that was not how Agnes and Yvonne interpreted my message. Within the hour, I was called into a closed-door meeting with both of them where I was berated and demeaned until I could no longer hold back the tears. I cried while they smiled. I felt like I was back in high school and the cool kids had cornered me.

This wasn't my first experience with grown bullies in the workplace, but definitely the worst. I stood up for myself when I was younger, but things had changed. I wasn't as secure in myself as I should have been. I didn't have the confidence to filter their comments and recognize they were ganging up on me because I was a threat. I was hard working, well-respected, and ambitious. They wanted me gone, because I knew their flaws and they knew my strengths. It took me years to realize they actually feared me.

They warned me before I left Agnes' office that if I told anyone what really happened in that meeting, they would make sure I left immediately. If I behaved and kept quiet, I could stay until the new position went into effect—seven more weeks. They wanted to make it look like I chose to leave, since they couldn't legally fire me. They told me not try to any more stunts like the email to the owners or I'd be officially fired for insubordination. I knew Agnes and Yvonne would be looking for any reason to make me leave early, so I had no choice but to comply with their rules.

I felt like I had just made a deal with the devil.

Ran into a Dead End

I needed those seven weeks to find a new job. The longest I went without a job previously was only a little more than a week, and that was when I was fired from the concrete company. How was I going to explain to my family that I quit my job when my husband was out of work? I wasn't fired, and it wasn't my intent to turn down the only job they were offering.

I felt so scared and hopeless.

I spent the next two months applying for every advertising, marketing, or purchasing job with the word manager in the title. My new plan was to leave the department store earlier than Jan. 28th with a better job offer than the coordinator position they had suggested. I wanted to leave because I had a better offer, not because I didn't have a choice in the matter.

That was the goal, at least.

Unlike my previous employment searches, great opportunities weren't falling in my lap. Windsor is an automotive city, and the local job market was still in rough shape due to the economic downturn that crushed our city three years prior. The classifieds had a few dozen job advertisements, in a city with thousands of educated and unemployed applicants. I applied for everything from advertising sales manager to managing a retail store. I wanted management, but as time progressed I knew I would settle for the first job that was offered.

My other coping strategy was to prove how valuable I was to Yvonne and Agnes, so maybe they would change their minds. Yet again, I foolishly went above and beyond to meet and exceed my duties for the first two weeks. However it didn't take long for me to realize that it didn't matter what I did. My career at the department store was officially over.

I did everything I could to set up the next person for success, since I wasn't willing to sacrifice my solid reputation out of anger. Most people at the department store respected my work ethic, and I didn't want to change their opinion before I left.

After seven weeks of trying to act normal while attempting to maintain my fleeting career at the store, reality finally sunk in. I had two days left and found out I would be spending them training my replacement. They finally hired someone to replace me.

This news sparked two crucial thoughts. The first thought was that I would no longer be a Baumann's employee. The fact that I was about to start over again was inevitable, and it terrified me. The second thing that occurred to me was that they actually trusted me to train my successor.

How could they trust me when they knew I didn't want to leave the company, and they were the ones forcing me out?

Most bosses wouldn't leave a new employee with someone they had just recently screwed over. Agnes and Yvonne were smart businesswomen who knew how to keep people in check. They also knew I had integrity and was loyal to the company. They knew I wouldn't jeopardize my reputation or sink to their level. They could trust me with the new employee, because they knew I would do the right thing.

I was finally starting to recognize that I wasn't forced out due to my inabilities; they wanted me gone because of my capabilities. I was capable of creating change. The other people at the department store respected me and listened to me. I didn't realize I had that power at that time in my life, but I did. Thankfully I've since realized the value of my voice, or this book would never have been published.

Every part of my career was essential to my success, especially the difficult parts that I thought would break me. Training my replacement was unbearable. It wasn't the trainee's fault. She was smart, experienced, and kind. I could tell she would be good at it. Although I also had a feeling she would hate it. She seemed genuine and helpful. Those traits would not be appreciated by her managers at Baumann's.

It tore me up inside to act like I was happy I was leaving, when I was crying on the inside. The people I worked with felt like family members. I'd wanted to retire from Baumann's. I still wanted to stay, despite the way Agnes and Yvonne treated me. That speaks volumes of the other 200-plus people who worked there. My longest and most positive work experience was over, and there was nothing I could do to change it.

I was forced to say my final good-bye, and I couldn't confide in my coworkers for support. I can admit now that I did spill the beans to a few people at the store, the few I fully trusted, but I lied to many people whom I still considered my friends. I was choking back tears constantly throughout the day.

Everyone reading this story will be exceptionally surprised to learn who my greatest comfort at work was, during those last emotionally-draining weeks of employment. It was actually Yvonne. She was sympathetic, compassionate, and cheered on my employment search. Deep down she knew the truth, and encouraged me to find the bright side in all of it.

"You'll find something better. It will all work out. I know this is hard for you because you are so emotionally attached to the store, but you'll find another job you love."

I'm sure her comments were partially due to guilt for the role she played in my sudden job loss, but I honestly believed she cared about me. We became quite close over the last few months I was there, and I believed she at least liked me as a person.

In hindsight, I owe her and Agnes a huge thank you. She was right about finding another job I loved. I needed this tragic ending to happen; otherwise I never would have written my first or second book. I would have been content to work at the department store in an entry-level position until I retired at sixty-five.

That simply was not my destiny.

After I left, I shared the truth about what happened to me with a few senior employees. Some of these employees still work at Baumann's, so I can't reveal their position, but they had significant experience and authority within the company. They informed me that I was not the first employee to be forced out by Agnes. I had witnessed many dramatic exits by other employees over the course of the last five years and was now learning that most of them had not been the employee's choice.

I can recall one incident in particular, when the store manager "quit." I personally witnessed an ugly argument between him and Agnes, and then he was suddenly gone. He left the store and didn't return. The former president—who had retired when I first started—came into work the following day, and met with Agnes in a closed-door meeting. An email went out soon after, informing us that the store manager had resigned. My sources at Baumann's were now telling me it had not been his decision to quit.

The problem was bigger than just me. Discovering that I wasn't the only one increased my confidence in my own abilities. I now knew I wasn't to blame for losing my job. I'm not completely innocent, and I should have stood my ground, but I took comfort knowing that many others had fallen into the same trap. I didn't feel quite as foolish.

A few months after I left, I sent the president of Baumann's and his younger brother (whom I knew Agnes treated poorly) a letter explaining exactly what happened to me there. I figured they had a right to know the truth, and could possibly dethrone the "queen of mean" before she verbally abused any more of their good employees.

I was working on rebuilding my self-esteem, and feeling determined that I could at least change things for future employees. I still had some doubt, so I shared the letter with a few friends from the department store prior to sending it. They all agreed that it didn't make me sound like a bitter ex-employee, and I had a right to send it.

I decided the safest bet was to mail the letter to their home address, which I fortunately found in the phonebook. I was too nervous that the mail would be intercepted if I sent it directly to the department store. Agnes was powerful and merciless. I didn't want to find out what she would do if she knew I was going over her head. I still remember hesitating for a few minutes before dropping the envelopes in the mailbox. She was no longer my boss, but I still lived in fear of her. Thankfully I no longer fear her now. I realize she's a woman just like me, flawed.

Dear Sean & Ryan,

It is with sincere sadness that my career at your fantastic store has come to an end. You and your family have always shown real appreciation and respect for your employees. I have felt it, and I have been blessed to have shared it with so many incredible co-workers. I will always speak highly of your business. It is because of this sincere belief, that you do care about your employees, that I feel the need to advise you of an issue within your company.

I am honestly not sure who is the direct root or bears responsibility, so I would rather just summarize a few issues and allow you to come to your own conclusion. I send this with the best intentions, because it genuinely pains me to leave on bad terms and I am not someone who wants to cause trouble. I also decided to put it in writing, so I am liable, because I assure you that I understand the defamation of character laws. My reputation is important to me.

The first few years working under Agnes seemed to go really well. I heard a lot of negative talk about Agnes from others. I felt she was tough but fair. I was impressed by how she'd worked her way up. I wanted to learn everything I could from her, and I followed every direction blindly.

It started coming up in my reviews that I was not vocalizing my opinions, showing leadership or pushing myself. My first two reviews were mostly positive, but I needed to be more assertive. I felt this assessment was fair, and I started making serious improvements. When Yvonne's position became available, I applied but I still lacked the confidence at that time to get it. I also agreed on that, but I was puzzled by why Maria wasn't given the opportunity.

I realized if I was going to get ahead, I needed to stand out. When we had the meeting for the new incentive program and we were quizzed afterwards, I won almost every prize. I joined the company newsletter, I participated in volunteer training programs, and I started questioning things I didn't agree on. I would question quantity changes to what we were buying and I even questioned decisions to drop certain SKUs.

I remember a specific time, when Yvonne was my manager and I questioned one of the new SKUs. She was still new, and she made it a

Leamington only SKU because the core fabric wasn't selling in Windsor. I told her it sold well in special orders and that the Windsor sales team was upset because we were dropping it. She said too late, it is now only available in Leamington. I ran EIS and I discovered it was the #1 selling sofa SKU in Windsor for custom orders. When I passed on my findings, Yvonne told me it was a waste of my time to research it, because Agnes made the decision to drop it and "since when is she ever going to change her mind?" I thought I was taking initiative and showing assertiveness. Instead I was spoken to with a complete lack of respect.

My role was incredibly chaotic and a significant amount of work had been added to the position since I'd started. They added the household cleaners, lamps, and accessories to every aspect of my job, which made it a constant juggling act. When something would fall through the cracks (which was very rare), I was either accused of spending too much time helping the sales staff or told I should be staying later to make sure everything is done. I was responsible for over 600 SKUs and I was expected to know the status of every order, or every SKU, at any given time. Unfortunately, sometimes I would miss something.

How about the other 99.8% of the time, when I was catching mistakes and solving problems? I stayed late now and then, when it was crucial. I even came in the day after the marathon, on a vacation day, to check the status of an advertised item. But I was scolded twice because I wanted to take the new store tags home to stuff them, rather than stay late to finish them at work. When I needed to take a second job because my husband was going back to school, I was first discouraged by Agnes and then by Yvonne. Both expressed concern that it would interfere with my productivity at work. I even went to see our human resources manager because I wanted to make sure I couldn't be punished for taking a waitressing position. Later when I dropped one of the hundreds of balls I was juggling, Yvonne suggested it was because I was working two jobs. The real reason is because I am human, and so is she.

Ask Barbara how many manual POs she gets from Yvonne that don't have a typing error. I found and corrected many of Yvonne's mistakes, but I felt I was not allowed to make any without her pointing it out. Next, the art director position became available. It was my second dream job within the entire company, and only second to the position of director of marketing and purchasing. My career started at a local advertising agency (project coordinator), then I created and sold ads for Businesses of Windsor magazine before I was partners in an ad agency for three years. I've even designed flyers for our competitors.

I thought the interview went well, but it was obvious the questions were directed to bring out my weaknesses. The HR manager didn't look at my portfolio or ask me about the list of marketing ideas I brought with me; she was focused on my lack of leadership experience.

How can I gain leadership experience, if it takes leadership experience to get a leadership role? I could feel that the interview was just a courtesy and I wasn't going to be given the chance. Agnes had a meeting with me afterwards, and said she felt that my "nice" disposition would be shattered by the directors. The former art director had warned me about the same thing. He said directors are encouraged to backstab and bring dirt in on each other, which he knew is not my style. It seemed Agnes was confirming that I was "too nice" for the role. When I talked to Yvonne afterwards about my disappointment, she seemed very understanding. She said, "Well, you know Agnes. Once she develops an opinion on someone, there is no changing it."

Then in March, I got a bad review. I received high scores on my first three reviews, especially in regards to my communication skills. That time, Yvonne gave me a one out of four for communication. She also gave specific examples of things that "weren't done," that had actually been done. The entire review came as a severe shock and I cried through most of it.

Yvonne crossed out a portion of the review during the review, because I reminded her I had proof it was inaccurate. My tears turned to anger and I started researching specific examples. I had (and still have), physical proof that the review was inaccurate. I went to HR the next day and showed her everything. The HR manager agreed with me, and she suggested that I take my concerns to Agnes.

Surprisingly, Agnes showed no interest in hearing my side. I was accused of being insubordinate and put on probation. I was given three months, with weekly training by Yvonne, to work on my weak areas as punishment for my insubordination. Amazingly, almost immediately my communication skills improved and by the time the three months were up I was new and improved again. Yvonne apologized for putting me through it, and implied Agnes was the one responsible for my bad review.

Despite the shocking review, I took responsibility and I admitted that I could do better. I started coming up with ideas and time saving suggestions. This was also when I was training for the marathon and building my confidence. It didn't matter if I agreed with Yvonne, I would share my opinion and then do whatever she asked of me. For months things were going really well. Then we were told about the changes in our department and how our roles would be divided in half. I immediately knew I wanted the challenge and creativity of the sales and marketing specialist position, but I knew Agnes and Yvonne saw me as a purchasing coordinator.

A purchasing coordinator needs to be highly organized, which I am. To be honest, Bill is not. I knew I would have to step up and prove I was a strong analytical thinker, highly determined to succeed and deserving of the sales and marketing specialist position to even be considered, which I feel I did in my interview. I researched work examples from the last year and put together a presentation for the internal interview (which I can send you).

When I was offered the purchasing coordinator position instead, I was obviously disappointed. Once again, I expressed my disappointed to Yvonne and she seemed sympathetic. Since I had the next day off work, I asked if I could go home and think about it before signing the contract for the new position. I told Yvonne I love this company, but I can't help but feel like I am never going to move up.

As Yvonne said, once Agnes has an opinion, there is no changing her mind. Yvonne suggested sales. She said, "Agnes commented on how well you sold yourself in the sales & marketing specialist interview, so what about sales?" Yvonne told me to talk to Paul, so I did. Our store's sales manager was excited and thought I would make a great salesperson. So, I went home and enjoyed my day off, thinking about my new career in sales. I was the leading salesperson for Businesses of Windsor magazine, so I felt this was a great fit.

The next morning, Yvonne insists on my resignation. Yvonne told me after the doubt I'd expressed for the purchase coordinator role, she couldn't give it to me. She then told me she needed my resignation by the next morning, so she could fill my role. I said I needed to think about it and would let her know in the morning. I told her about my interview with Paul, and that I was following her suggestion. Yvonne then had a closed-door meeting with Agnes, which was followed by Agnes having a closed-door meeting with Paul. Those meetings resulted in a staged interview, designed to make me look like I'm only interested in sales as a way to escape Yvonne.

Which is completely untrue!

I've learned to work quite well with Yvonne, and I wouldn't risk my job over personality differences. I can work with anyone. The next day, Yvonne called me into the office and requested my resignation letter. I told her it was not ready and instead I sent out the email that you saw. My only intent in that email was to A: keep my job until the end of January, so I could find a new one, B: thank both of you for having such a great company, and C: hopefully land the sales position. That was my only intent, and that is fact.

Instead I was asked into Agnes's office for a closed-door meeting with Yvonne (once again, no HR representative). I was accused of sending the email as a back-handed slap against Yvonne. I have read that email numerous times; there is no attack on Yvonne. They were only upset that I copied both of you on it. I was told I was not allowed to say anything to anyone about what happened, or I would be immediately dismissed. Otherwise, I could stay until Jan. 28th. Agnes cut me off and did not give me an opportunity to say what really happened. The number of your current employees who approached me about staying has been overwhelming. Everyone was asking me to stay, and

I couldn't even tell them it wasn't my choice to leave. These are close friends, and I couldn't share what I am going through with them. After talking with some past and some current management, I've learned that I am not the first to be squeezed out.

The new art director told me the previous director didn't choose to leave, but that was how they made it look to everyone else. The dark side to this business is not for me. I would never have survived management when Agnes was running things, so she was right not to promote me.

However, that is unfortunate for your company since anywhere else would benefit from my leadership. I use a team mentality, positive reinforcement and my own hard work, to get things done. I don't believe intimidation, fear-based control techniques, and negative reinforcement build good employees. Look at the low turnover rate in the warehouse, accounting, credit, and customer care. Look at the high turnover rate in management, sales leadership, purchasing, and marketing positions. Look at how few in my area have been promoted. The evidence is there. Hopefully you can create positive change before you lose more good employees.

Sincerely,

Jenn

I assume the letters were read, but I didn't receive any type of response from either brother. Mailing those letters made me feel better about the situation, because I did my part to resolve it. I brought the problem to the attention of those who should have had the power to fix it. The burden was no longer on my shoulders.

I knew it wasn't possible to revive my career at the department store and I needed to move forward for the sake of both my financial and mental wellbeing. I was collecting unemployment and doing a little freelance copywriting on the side, but I needed to find steady employment fast.

A Whole New Direction

I decided to combine my past waitressing experience with my professional business experience by applying for management roles in the hospitality industry. My previous manager at the private golf course taught me a lot about proper server etiquette, and I felt confident my outgoing personality would be an asset in any customer service position. Most food and beverage management roles also involved monitoring inventory and purchasing food and beverages based on fluctuating needs, which would be very similar to my role at the department store.

I went on about a half dozen interviews during my last few weeks at Baumann's, and a few more during the first week I was on unemployment assistance. However, responses to my resume slowed down to a complete halt in the second week of my unemployment. I had second interviews scheduled for a salesperson position at a furniture store and an assistant manager at a golf course, but my options were looking slim.

My crooked career path gave me plenty of interviewing experience, but my confidence was lacking. I also had to lie on every interview, which is not one of my strong suits. I couldn't accurately explain how my last job ended without sounding like a crazy person, so I developed a believable cover story. I told potential employees that Baumann's did some restructuring and downsizing, which eliminated my position. I told interviewers that the timing was perfect, because I was ready for a managerial role. Although I thought it sounded acceptable and was true for the most part,

I was still worried that I would be caught in a lie and ruin my chances of future employment.

I spent a lot of time quietly panicking. I acted confident and positive in front of everyone except Rachel. She knew my weaknesses and insecurities, and never judged me for them. She also was the only one to know that I started smoking cigars. Prior to losing my dream job, I had smoked one cigarette and one cigar over the course of the last eighteen months. During my six weeks without a job, I smoked two packs of cigars.

It's a habit that I still fight. I can go a couple months without any, and then smoke a pack of eight cigars in one week. I purposely sign myself up for different races and marathons to force myself to quit, and then after weeks or months of cigar-free training, I celebrate my success with a cigar. It's one of my dirty little secrets. I have inspired people to quit smoking, and sometimes I feel like I'm a fraud for my weakness. I haven't had one recently, so maybe putting my secret in print will help ensure that my last cigar is actually my last cigar. I'm not going to beat myself up for it either way. We all have our vices. They key is ensuring you are the one controlling the addiction instead of the addiction controlling you.

After six nerve-racking weeks without a job, I finally found a wonderful position with the word manager in the title. I had a second interview at the golf course mid-February, then they called me in to offer me the position four weeks later. Unfortunately the job wouldn't start immediately, since it wasn't golf season yet. My start date kept getting postponed. The anticipation and additional delay was shaking my already fragile confidence.

The longer I went without working, the more I worried. I was scared something would happen and the job offer would no longer be available, so I continued my search and went on two more interviews. I was even offered another job, but it didn't have the word manager in the title. I was ready to lead and had my heart set on the Assistant Manager position at the golf course. I just needed to have faith that it would work out. Fortunately, it did.

Once I finally started my new job, my confidence was rejuvenated and stronger than ever. I finally got my wish. I had an opportunity to gain management experience and prove myself as a competent leader. I was determined to be the best Assistant Manager that Windsor's finest golf course had ever seen. I was ready to prove Agnes wrong!

My main function would be managing the waitstaff, re-ordering alcohol and confectionary items based on demand, and coordinating various details for club events. This golf course had a stellar reputation throughout the city, and was considered the most prominent location for high-end weddings in Southern Ontario. I knew it would be challenging, but I was overjoyed to have the chance to test my leadership skills.

The gentleman they hired to be the Food and Beverage Manager had significant experience, but seemed frantic right from the beginning. He was running himself ragged, trying to ensure that we were ready for the start of the golf season. The food and beverage aspect of the business was in the early stages of new management, and almost everyone on the staff still needed to be hired and trained.

However, we didn't have any training manuals. The Food and Beverage Manager hadn't had a chance to put together any sort of training plan for the new staff. We were lucky the Assistant Manager of the Golf Course's Pro Shop was experienced with the point-of-sale system, and had her own manuals that we could use to train the waitstaff.

I did my best to help him train all of the new employees, create the schedules, and manage our inventory levels, but he still couldn't keep up with his responsibilities. We were constantly having emergencies and mishaps that contradicted the club's polished reputation.

What made the problem even worse was that my new boss had a tendency to disappear during important functions. A manager needs to be accessible during a wedding, sizeable golf tournament, or large corporate affair to ensure that every guest's needs are being met. It was a high-class establishment, with high prices and even higher expectations.

After a few short months, it became apparent to everyone that the manager was hiding something. We suspected a drinking problem, but didn't have the evidence to support our suspicion. The General Manager and Head Chef had to make the difficult decision to let him go.

The timing couldn't have been worse.

We were at the start of a busy golf and wedding season, and most of the staff was just as new as me. Surprisingly, that didn't stop the General Manager and Head Chef from offering me his position. I was already handling the majority of the workload, so it seemed like their plan might work. It would be on a trial basis, and both would be available to support me. I also had the help of the establishment's experienced Client Service Manager, who had an exceptional talent for coordinating major events without a hiccup.

I went from being offered a low-level coordinating position at a company where I thought I'd proven myself, to being offered a high-level management position at a place I'd only worked for a couple of months. Pretty odd, when you think about it. I was suddenly a manager, of thirty employees at a lavish event facility.

It was lucky for me that it ended up being one of the best learning experiences of my life, especially when it came to the general manager of the golf course. He had a sincere passion for superior customer service and an effective management style. It was the exact example I needed, after my experience at the department store.

Speaking of Baumann's, a few months into my chaotic, yet rewarding managerial position, I received a surprising message on Facebook from someone who wasn't even on my contact list. The message was eerily familiar.

Hi Jenn,

I'm not sure if you'll remember me. I'm Deanna, the girl you trained for 2 days at Baumann's. The reason I am emailing you is that I would LOVE to discuss a few problems I have been having there....I don't really know where else to turn, because my boss, Cathy, has left abruptly. She was the only one who had been sympathetic with my excessive workload and unrealistic requests by a certain person, but is now gone. I am now on my own and have kind of been threatened recently. I also remember you telling me a few things before you left, and I think you were trying to warn me. I hope I'm not imposing. I was hoping to get some insight from you. Thank you for your time.

Deanna

My heart started to race. Self-doubt had started to burrow its way into my head since leaving the store, and I'd started to think that maybe I was just too weak to handle the pressure at Baumann's. Maybe Agnes was right about me. I was running myself ragged trying to accomplish all of my new management responsibilities. Maybe Agnes knew me better than I knew myself? Maybe I was victimizing myself, and their abuse wasn't as severe as I interpreted it to be. I was constantly fighting various insecurities because of Agnes' and Yvonne's devastating comments and behavior towards me. Now I know the mistreatment that I felt when I worked there was actually real. Agnes and Yvonne had a new victim, and she was reaching out to me.

> Hi Deanna,
> I'm surprised to hear from you, but not surprised at the topic. I do remember you and I DO sympathize!! Remember when I said I loved 98% of the people at the department store? Well, it is true! There is an amazing, supportive staff there, with two exceptions. Unfortunately, the exceptions rule that world. Those exceptions manipulated things into making it look like I quit. I was warned that if I said anything to anyone, they would make my exit immediate & ugly. If you've been threatened in anyway, it will continue—and most likely get worse.
> I tried to work with them and I tried to work against them to change it. I did what I could when I was there, and then I tried again after I left, hoping no one else would be treated the way I was treated. Nothing changed, and I doubt anything will. I wasn't the first; you just proved I wasn't the last! Lay low, do what they say, and look for a new job, because it probably won't get better. I am sorry I couldn't say anything back then to really warn you.
> I know it's not what you want to hear, but karma has a way of making it all work out. I now have a wonderful job, making more money with really supportive, amazing bosses. I truly wish the same for you!
> And you are not imposing. I understand, and I am willing to talk if you need it.
> Sincerely,
> Jenn

Deanna responded almost immediately.

> Hi Jenn,
> OK, what a relief, to hear that I am not going crazy...Isn't it funny how two bullies can work together like that? That is so SAD that they made you tell people you quit...how did they do that? I am definitely looking, but you know how hard things are. I have excelled in all of my jobs and was doing OK, until Cathy "left"...and she protected me...but now that she's gone, it's been hell...it was actually hell then too, but I could go to her and say I can't do it...I still had a hard time keeping up, but she backed me up.
> Seriously, if I made a lot of money I would consider staying there, but I make the lowest money I have made in 20 years! I wanted experience and to move up...I have never been so stressed in my life...this has never happened to me before....I feel like I should be learning from this...but every day I am screwed more than the day before! And the condescending emails!!! Wow....oh, after you left, they all had some kind of training for 2 weeks! I was on my own...nice...Agnes just had me in her office for an hour, insulting me and telling me to admit they hired the wrong person and I am not the one for the job...I wouldn't admit it...but I kept my cool....then the next day, she called me in w/ Yvonne and told me in front of her that my performance was unacceptable....They freak me out...did you ever go to HR, or did they corner you?
> Thanks so much for responding...this is helping me feel better!
> Deanna

Deanna and I chatted back and forth for the next few weeks. I advised her that it would be better to find a new job than to waste time and energy trying to change things at Baumann's. Thankfully, she was soon able to.

Unfortunately, I was now experiencing the stress and burden of my new job. Although I liked what I was doing and got along with pretty much everyone, the demanding schedule and overwhelming responsibilities were taking their toll on me. I was working fifty to sixty hours a week, and constantly having to answer my cellphone during my limited free time. My role as food and beverage manager was consuming my life.

Headed in the Wrong Direction

I t got worse at the end of the summer because we were hosting a national tournament and expecting a significant number of spectators. It took weeks of detailed meetings and brainstorming to figure out how our facility, which usually caters to a few hundred people a day, would be able to handle the needs of a few thousand.

I worked 68 hours the week before the tournament.

The week of the tournament was even more draining than the planning. We were serving customers from two stationary beverage carts, our concession stand, and the restaurant, which we expanded for the event. We also had breakfast for the golfers and lunch for volunteers, every day for the entire week of the tournament.

My staff was stretched thin and I was running around like a crazy woman trying to make sure everyone had enough beer and alcohol to serve the masses. I actually have a pretty funny story that took me back to one of my first professional jobs.

I ripped my dress to my waistline.

Seriously, how does that happen to the same person twice?

God must know I can take a joke.

On the first day of the tournament, I wore a fitted, A-line dress with a small slit in the back. I was in the fridge with the chef and a waitress when I bent over to grab a case of beer from the floor. My slit split and went far

76

enough up that my bare white butt was exposed to both of them. I quickly grasped it closed and asked the waitress to get me a skirt from the golf shop. Of course I was embarrassed that both of my co-workers saw such an unpleasant side of me, but I got over it quickly. I knew it would just be another funny story I could later tell about my strange career history.

I ended up working 72 hours that week. In my exhaustion, I let something slip by me. I missed an instruction on an event's work order the day after the tournament, and it cost the club a few hundred dollars. I felt horrible about the mistake and frustrated that I ended up failing under the pressure.

Maybe Agnes was right about me after all, and I wasn't management material. It's a thought that has entered my head a hundred times since I was forced to leave the department store. It crossed my mind when I had to fire a waitress for stealing, and I could barely get the words out. Her harsh judgement of my abilities forced me to follow through every time I had to make a smart business decision that would negatively impact my staff.

Agnes knew my weaknesses and my undeniable people-pleasing nature, which was still my greatest professional fault. I tried so hard to prove her wrong, but I struggled to delegate work and wasn't effective when it came to disciplining the staff for their oversights.

Abuse has a lasting effect. I still experience the same mental anguish over my ex-boyfriend's comments about my weight. I have a hard time believing that I'm not fat, even when I'm in the best shape of my life. That's why it's hard to believe I'm strong enough to be a good manager, even when I'm actually doing it.

Verbal abuse lingers and it's very hard to shake the self-doubt.

Fortunately, I'm not a quitter. I used that incident to push myself to try harder. I was proud of my job, and didn't want to lose it. I continued to work crazy hours to show I was deserving of such grand responsibilities. I took their criticism and advice seriously, so I could develop into the manager I knew I was meant to be.

We successfully wrapped up the first hectic golf season, which was immediately followed by more weddings, showers, and countless over-the-top holiday parties. I was still averaging close to 60 hours a week, and desperately needed a vacation.

Working so many hours gave me a chance to save up some money, so I treated my husband and myself to our first vacation since our honeymoon, six years prior. We went on an exciting, all-inclusive trip to Jamaica that included hiking and zip-lining through the forest. There is something absolutely freeing about flying at insane speeds through the wilderness. Spending that quality time with my husband was a sweet, yet short-lived taste of how I wanted to live my life.

I received a similar feeling of freedom five months later, but it was also short-lived. Surprisingly, it started with a bad day that got significantly worse. I took a drive to my favorite running spot, so I could clear my head surrounded by fresh air and Mother Nature.

When I finished running and went to get into my car, I noticed glistening pieces of glass on the passenger seat. I also noticed various items from inside my car had been tossed about, and my glove box was open. Someone had broken my window and taken off with a bag containing spare work clothes (I learned from the ripped skirt incidents and always carried back up clothing), my dress shoes, and my purse. My purse had my wallet and both my work and personal cellphones in it. I was robbed while running.

I approached a few strangers, looking for someone with a cellphone, so I could call the police. I finally found help from two other victims. Their cars were left unlocked and ransacked, but nothing was missing. They kept their cars empty. I tucked my purse under the seat and locked my door, which obviously wasn't a good enough strategy. I've learned from that life lesson and now only carry my driver license and bank card on my person when I plan on going for a run.

The other people helped me search the forested area for my stuff and we were able to find my work shoes and the bag they were in. We also found my purse, but it was empty. A few hours after I got home and reported my credit cards as stolen, a man and his young daughter knocked on my door. She found my wallet at a park and wanted to return it to me. Everything except the cash (which was minimal) was still inside.

I'm so grateful for the kindness of strangers.

Losing my work cellphone was freeing! I had about sixty hours without it and it was the happiest I'd felt since my vacation to Jamaica. My work life stopped interrupting my rare free time with my family and friends, and I loved every minute of it.

However, the cellphone was necessary for my job. My thoughtful boss made sure to replace it as quickly as possible. I made the decision not to replace my personal cellphone, because I rarely used it. It actually took me more than two years to get a new one, long after I eagerly returned the cellphone that came with the food and beverage manager's position back to the golf club. I'm not a fan of cellphones, and rarely use the one I have now.

After one of the longest and most grueling weeks at the golf course, I finally had a free Saturday night. Saturday nights off were rare, since we were booked almost every weekend for a wedding. This Saturday was only free because a wedding had been cancelled a few weeks prior. Although I felt bad the couple's plans to marry had perished, I was ecstatic that I wouldn't be spending another Saturday with my work family. I leaped at the chance to get the evening off and made sure to schedule myself for the earliest shift possible.

Crossing Paths
with the Past

I made plans to get together with an old friend from the department store and Deanna, the woman who replaced me at Baumann's, who had later contacted me when she was experiencing threats and abuse. We had some pressing matters to discuss, since more drama had been unfolding at my former employer. Deanna had informed me that her replacement was now being mistreated, and had contacted her for advice.

The cycle of abuse continues.

Deanna had contacted me on Facebook a few weeks prior about the current situation. The new victim, Helen, was now feeling the full force of Agnes and Yvonne's bullying, and she didn't know what to do. Unfortunately, I thought I might be able to help. I was certain that if the president knew that it was more than just Deanna and I, he'd finally do something to rectify the problem. The new woman in our role had an inspirational backstory of overcoming tough odds and building a successful future for herself. He may not care what happened to me, but surely he would care about what helped to this sweet, young woman.

The verbal and mental abuse Deanna experienced was still very fresh, and her initial reaction was somewhat less than professional. She sent a lengthy, detailed letter to the wives of the owners, informing them of what their husbands were allowing to take place at their company. She shared what she sent with me, and I felt her tactic came on too strong to be effective. I didn't know her well at the time, although she is definitely a friend now, and I didn't want to be associated with personal attacks and threats. That's simply not my style.

My reputation still mattered to me. A different friend from Baumann's had recently informed me there was a rumor going around that Deanna and I were trying to bring the company down. People were saying that we were personally attacking the Baumann family, and threatening a lawsuit. I still cared about many people who worked there, so I felt the need to set the record straight.

I sent an email in an attempt to finally fix the problem, while warning them that the problem still existed. I'm a writer, which means I always assume I can fix a bad situation with a carefully composed letter.

Sean & Ryan,

I honestly believe I left your company on good terms, despite what happened to me, and I want to make sure that rumors of my involvement in inappropriate personal attacks are put to rest. I still talk to numerous close friends at your department store and some feel that my relationship with Deanna may be tarnishing my reputation.

Deanna did contact me in September because she felt she was being mistreated and that Yvonne and Agnes appeared to be forcing her out. She remembered that when I trained her, I kept saying that I loved 98% of the staff, but I wouldn't tell her who I considered the other 2%. I said I loved my job and I was having a hard time leaving my work family. She also remembers me crying uncontrollably on my last day, which she felt was odd because everyone was under the impression that I "chose" to leave.

Back then, she asked me why I was leaving when I didn't have a new job, and my answer sounded like bullshit (because I was lying). She always knew something wasn't right with my "quitting." After the bullying began for Deanna, she started thinking that maybe I went through it too, maybe that was why I left or I was possibly forced out, maybe those two were the 2% I wouldn't tell her about. I also think some of the sales staff let it slip to make her feel like she wasn't alone in what she was going through. They were all very supportive of me. Anyway, she found me on Facebook and sent a message seeking my advice.

I told her if she felt they were trying to push her out, then her best bet was to find a new job and move on. I sent several message advising her to move on. It won't change, don't try to fix it, just get out before it gets worse. She said she wasn't sleeping, took up smoking again and was nauseous constantly. She dreaded going to work. She needed to get out of there, because it was clear she couldn't handle it and it was affecting every aspect of her life. I told her not to go to HR, but she did anyway. HR turned it against her. The same thing happened to me. I'd warned her that HR was not neutral. I explained what happened to me and said she should give two weeks' notice, and leave on good terms.

She didn't listen; she was angry and wanted revenge. I told her that contacting both of you was her only hope for justice (I thought maybe if you heard it from someone else, you might start realizing it's all true), but she sent it to everyone's wives. I told her NO personal attacks and NO accusations she could not prove in writing. I don't know what she has proof of from her letter, but I know she was out of line with her attacks. I said be the bigger person and leave with your head up high, but she didn't listen. I said that you can warn them what is going on, but you can't force them to fix it. I have evidence to support my advice to her, and I sincerely wished she would have handled it better.

However, she was driven to irrational behavior and she is not the only one who should be held accountable. It is not what she did, but what drove her to do it that needs to be examined. She said she called you (Sean) several times on her last day, but you did not return her call. Is that true? Did you send her a letter from a lawyer, saying she should have contacted you directly? If she left you messages, then she did contact you directly, and was ignored.

I sent both of you letters directly, but I did not get a response. There were no changes to how employees were treated because of my letter and I still have proof to support every word in it, including my blatantly inaccurate employee review. You never asked for my proof? There is an obvious issue, just look at the lengthy list of victims...why did these people leave (those who had a choice)?

I recently read this great book, *Monday Morning Manager*, and the author said "people quit people, not jobs." It also talks about how the right employees are the greatest assets and the wrong employees are your greatest liabilities. I highly recommend the book for every manager.

It is in my best interests not to contact you so I don't get dragged into any mess that Deanna may have caused, but I keep thinking I will touch your conscience somehow. A part of me still believes you are good people, but it fades with every story I hear of someone else being mistreated. I feel horrible that I walked away without changing things, and allowed someone else to suffer through it. I feel guilty about what happened to Cathy and Deanna and what is still happening to other people who are still there, but I wasn't the one causing the abuse and I am not the owner allowing the abuse to continue. I am not the one who should feel bad.

Also, just so you are aware, there is a new target since Deanna left. Someone else in that department directly under the same two people is now feeling the pressure and bullying. It won't stop until someone takes it seriously. Please do not hesitate to contact me if you want proof for the purpose of justice on anything I've written in this letter, or the previous letter. I may not be a victim anymore, but I'd feel better knowing that NO ONE was a victim anymore.

Sincerely,

Jenn

The president of the store, Sean, called me at home a few hours after I sent the email. He wanted to discuss my email and the evidence I had. He sounded so sincere and agreed with me that there was an obvious problem. He promised me that he would not tell Agnes or Yvonne what I had shared with him, and that he'd be in touch as soon as he could. I warned him that Helen would be fired if they found out she spoke with Deanna, and he assured me that he would not let that happen.

I shed light on a problem and someone was taking it seriously. It was a huge confidence boost and renewed my faith in Baumann's. The family image they portrayed finally felt legitimate again.

I was pleased that it sounded like my pleas finally got through to him, so you can imagine my surprise when I discovered a few days later that Helen was let go from the department store. Helen told Deanna that Sean spoke with her and then with Agnes. This was immediately followed with Agnes and Yvonne deciding that Helen's performance was not up to par, and her contract wouldn't be renewed. Agnes made a comment warning Helen that she shouldn't associate with former employees.

I was furious! I felt completely betrayed and I couldn't hold my anger in.

Sean,

I guess I was wrong for trusting that you wanted to make things better for your employees. Helen was fired today, and it is my fault for believing that you could put an end to the bullying and inexcusable treatment of people in that department. Will it ever end? Do you think that department store is ever going to run successfully if it's constantly training new people?

Agnes and Yvonne can keep their jobs while people like Helen and myself have ours ripped out from under us because we spoke up against the bullying? IT IS NOT LEGAL! Is that the reputation you want for Baumann's? I chose not to contact the local media or lawyers, or take this public in any way, because of my respect and appreciation for you and your family. Helen losing her job just made me lose that respect completely.

My proof of foul play is undeniable. If you won't take this problem seriously, then I will find someone willing to listen and do something about it.

I am still well-liked by and influential to the majority of your employees, and there is strength in numbers. I am in marketing and I know how to use social media to my advantage. I am sure Deanna and Helen will help this cause and it won't be hard to recruit more past (maybe current) employees. If you won't fix the mess, then I will fix it for Shane, Will, David, Cathy, Deanna and now Helen. Oh, I forgot Sarah in HR. She spoke up for

Deanna and then her contract wasn't renewed. Not a coincidence! I bet if I dig deep enough, I will learn there were plenty more before us.

Agnes is a paranoid control freak, willing to sacrifice anyone who she feels is a threat to her personal agenda. She trained me that she was the one who ran that company, not you or Ryan, which I now see is true. I am done waiting for Baumann's to do something about it. All you did was make it worse, and it cost another good person another good job.

If Helen doesn't have her job back by tomorrow at noon (and I mean a job where she doesn't have to work for Agnes or Yvonne), then I will make it my very public mission to get it back for her. I know you can't do anything about it, so you can expect me in the store tomorrow afternoon to kick off my mission.

Sincerely,
Jenn

Wow! Rereading that email now empowers and frightens me. It took guts and foolishness to write that to the president of my former company. I've never been so angry and let it take over. Of course, I realized immediately after I hit send that I let my emotions get the better of me. My email was very out of character. It reminded me of the horrible email I sent at the concrete company.

I now practice the principle of type it, save it as a draft, wait a few hours, review, edit, and then send. If I'm really outraged over something and worried about damaging consequences, I'll send it to my close friends for their opinion. I've made a lot of mistakes in my life, so I always make a point of extracting a valuable lesson from each of my follies.

I never followed through on my threat, which wasn't a surprise to me. I genuinely cared for the majority of my co-workers and I didn't want to rage in a war against my former employer. I wanted justice for the never-ending list of victims, but I didn't really think I had the power to actually create change. If I couldn't convince the owner there was a problem, I probably couldn't convince anyone else.

My initial reaction was anger, because I felt somewhat responsible. I butted my nose in where it didn't need to be, and it cost someone their job. Now, I must point out that was how I felt at the time in my life when this was happening. I felt guilty because I spoke up and an innocent person lost their job. That is not how I feel now.

I recognize now that Helen reached out to Deanna because she was unhappy and not being treated properly. I was not the person treating her unfairly. I brought the situation to the attention of someone who should have had the power to resolve it. The responsible parties are the people who harassed her and then took away her job. I tried to help and ultimately it worked out for the best. She was no longer being demeaned and threatened. Leaving that company worked out quite well for both Deanna and I, so I'm sure things worked out just fine for her too.

Baumann's was my past and I was focused on my future.

I had a better job now, right?

I was enjoying a Saturday night with two wonderful women discussing a company that no longer had any hold over me. However, during our intense discussion about how the company had betrayed countless people who worked under the reign of Agnes, my cellphone rang. I ignored it at first because I needed an uninterrupted night of venting over wine with my friends, but ended up glancing down after a few minutes out of foolish curiosity. It was the chef at the golf course, and the email was the last straw at my current job. He was accusing me of accepting a bribe for turning on the air conditioner while the guests decorated the hall.

The mother of the girl whom the baby shower was thrown for gave me a generous tip for helping her organize and setup the event. I showed the chef the tip and her thank you card when I received it, because I was so touched by the gesture. Yes, the woman had asked me about turning on the air conditioning at night so her chocolates wouldn't melt, but the chef told me not to turn it on, so I didn't. I'm the type of an employee who always does what she is told.

His email was accusatory and as emotionally charged as my earlier email to Sean Baumann. I was too angry to respond and finally was wise enough to resist the urge. Fortunately, the general manager checked the programmable thermostat. It had been preprogrammed to come on, because we originally expecting to have a wedding that evening. The misunderstanding was clarified without an apology.

I originally booked the following day off work for my cousin's baby shower, but Chef insisted that I came in for the start of the client's baby shower, since I was the one who helped her plan it. The agreement was that I would stay until the meal was served and then another manager would be there until close. He waited until that morning to squash my plans.

"This is your event, and I expect you to stay until the end."

I was fed up by this point. I'd spent the last year-and-a-half devoted to this golf course. I was tired of putting his demands ahead of my family and myself. I was looking forward to attending my cousin's shower and I wasn't willing to accept no for an answer.

It was time for me to stand up for myself.

I called the banquet supervisor in and made sure she had everything she needed to finish off the day. I didn't ask if I could leave. I told him I was leaving. It was very out of character for me and completely contradicted my history of doing as I'm told. I didn't care, cause it felt good. At this point in my crooked career path I wasn't even concerned if my bold behavior cost me my job. I wanted to run as fast as I could from that demanding position, but needed a little time away to collect my thoughts and feelings.

I was fuming the entire way to the baby shower. I turned off my cellphone to ensure the chef wouldn't spoil my afternoon. Unfortunately, it wasn't the chef who ruined my cousin's shower. My sister-in-law was waiting for me at the front entrance. I could see sincere sadness in her eyes as I approached her.

"Is everything okay?"

"No. That was your brother. Your dad called him. Uncle Jeff was diagnosed with cancer."

I can't recall anything else she said. I couldn't believe it. Uncle Jeff had always been invincible, in my eyes. He was the rebellious, unmarried, and childless fun-loving uncle who had teased me relentlessly throughout most of my childhood. The news didn't seem real.

I sat through the baby shower for as long as I could before quietly sneaking out of the hall, after the last gift was opened. I needed to see my father. We weren't very close, but I thought he'd be devastated about his brother's diagnosis. My father didn't take bad news very well, and I wanted to be strong for him. I also wanted more details on how Uncle Jeff was doing.

My father and brother were standing in the driveway when I got there. I rushed to hug both and was unable to hold back my tears. My dad was calmer and more in control than I predicted. He said he just came from the hospital and the doctor said it was Leukemia. He also told us that my uncle didn't want any visitors. Thankfully, I have a fantastic habit of ignoring my father's advice, so after a short and unemotional visit with him, I went directly to the hospital. I rushed to my uncle's room as quickly as my feet could carry me.

"I know my dad said that you wouldn't really want company, but I had to see you."

"Why wouldn't I want company?"

"I don't know. That's just what he said."

"I was hoping for visitors. I hate being stuck in here."

"Well then, it's a good thing I never listen to him"

He smiled and sighed.

"I can't believe you're in here," I said.

"Me neither."

I asked him how he discovered something was wrong and what the doctors were saying. Neither sounded good, so I asked him about his most recent vacation. My uncle was always traveling somewhere tropical, and his stories of wild partying were legendary.

"You're making me jealous. I would love just to have one day off without my cellphone ringing."

"Then turn it off."

"I can't turn off my work phone! There is always someone who needs something, when I least expect it."

We spent the next hour discussing all the hours I was working and how stressed out I had become. I explained how physically draining it was to run around a massive golf club in high heels for sixty-something hours a week. I had no time to do anything fun. That's when my uncle asked me the critical question that would change my entire life's direction.

"I thought you were a writer. Why are you killing yourself at a golf course?"

"Good question!"

"Are you happy? Are you enjoying your life?"

Here is a man who has just received a serious cancer diagnosis, and he's asking me if I'm happy. I tried to change the conversation back to him, but he wouldn't let it go. I told him that I loved my husband, family, and friends, so therefore, I loved my life. I just didn't get to spend very much time with the people who mattered.

"What about earning a living as a writer? You've been writing impressive stuff since you were little. You're a smart girl. Figure out a way to make money doing what you love, and you'll always be happy."

Although my uncle did what he loved in his spare time, he did not love his job. He worked in an automotive factory for almost thirty years. My uncle was impatiently anticipating his retirement the following year, despite being only a few months shy of his fiftieth birthday. He was single and well paid, so he could afford the luxury of retiring early and celebrating his golden years while he was still healthy enough to really make the most of it.

He should have been healthy enough. He was an avid runner who regularly did high-intensity workout videos. He always teased me that he picked up girls half his age on vacation, which was certainly believable. My uncle looked at least ten years younger than he was, and he was very physically fit. The cancer was about to ruin that.

My uncle's advice lingered in my head long after I left the hospital. I wasn't enjoying my job, or appreciating its challenges as much as I had in the beginning. I hardly ever saw my friends and family, and my husband was handling the majority of the housework. My crazy schedule was significantly interfering with my "real" life.

Time to Change Directions

An incredibly daring thought came to me that night. Maybe I could make a living as a writer? I made a little money freelance writing online between the job at the department store and starting at the golf course. I saw hundreds of writing assignments advertised on the freelance website.

Could I make enough to live on from my writing?

I had a decent-sized chunk of debt that has been nearly impossible to pay down, and I was finally making a dent in it. I also just bought a car and took out a consolidation loan with a big weekly payment. When you added in my household bills, I desperately needed a steady income.

Fortunately my current job frustration and love of writing surpassed my financial concerns. I sent out a handful of online bids on the freelance website I had used a year and a half ago. I promised myself I would take another leap of faith and follow my dreams if anything positive came from my efforts.

Overnight, I was awarded three out of the six assignments I bid on. I gave my two weeks' notice the very next day. I was as nervous as I had been when I was suddenly forced from my job at Baumann's, but I was also ridiculously excited. I had the opportunity to make a living from home, as a writer. That is the only thing I've ever truly wanted from my life.

This was the ideal career choice for me, but I never considered it a possibility until my uncle suggested it. I'm lucky my wonderful husband was supportive of the idea, because it took some of the pressure off of me. We struggled financially when the factory he worked at for twenty years suddenly closed its doors. I had to take a second job back then, so we could manage our expenses. He knew this was important to me, and was willing to make any sacrifices necessary for me to fulfill my dream. Lasting couples lean on each other during times of uncertainty.

Chef decided I couldn't be trusted to finish my shifts or train my replacement, so I was able to still receive a paycheck for the next two weeks while writing from home. It allotted me the opportunity to build a small financial cushion that I wouldn't need to dip into until much later on.

I was actually making really good money the first few weeks I worked from home. I was earning more than I did as a manager and I wasn't working nearly as many hours. I had time to go for a run or to the gym in the morning, and was able to have dinner on the table each night when my husband came home from work. It also gave me the freedom to run to the hospital a few times during the week to check in on my uncle.

Visiting him was inspiring. My Uncle Jeff maintained his positive outlook and selfless nature through lengthy hospital stays and draining chemotherapy. His support and enthusiasm for my recent career endeavors fueled my determination.

Everything was going better than I'd imagined.

I've had this false sense of security before in my career, so I didn't want to put too much faith in it. However, I desperately wanted to see my best friend Rachel, who now lived six hours away. I hadn't had the chance to visit her when I was working all those crazy hours, and I was long overdue for a vacation. I was wrapping up a few projects and had just sent out a bunch of new bids. It was the perfect time to escape for a few days.

On the morning I was preparing to leave, God gave me some much-needed reassurance. I was concerned that the first batch of work was a fluke, and worried I wouldn't earn any new business. I have a tendency to doubt my abilities and I'm always looking for signs that I'm actually on the right path.

Fortunately, I was pleasantly surprised. I landed a large job that would almost cover my financial needs for the next two months. Receiving that news prior to going on vacation allowed me to enjoy my visit without worrying about work or money.

That feeling was even more freeing than zip lining or being cellphone free.

The trip to Rachel's cottage-style home in the forest was relaxing and wonderful, and I returned home to a summer's worth of exciting work. I was consistently landing new clients and receiving rave reviews, building a pretty solid profile as a copywriter.

I was finally feeling the joy of living without restraints.

I made my own schedule, determined my work load, and spent my free time as I saw fit. My stepchildren were practical grown and hardly ever around, my husband became self-sufficient when I was working all those crazy hours at the golf course, and I only had to take care of myself.

Life was better than I ever dreamt it could be and I couldn't imagine ever working a "real" job again. My uncle was right. I'm a writer. I love to write, and I'll be happy for the rest of my life if I can make a living doing what I love.

To be completely honest, although copywriting was an interesting form of writing, it wasn't truly the type of writing that I wanted to do. I wanted to write from the heart. I wanted to inspire and create powerful stories that empowered others. The assignments I was awarded were to write ad copy for realtors, skincare products, and garage door installers. I couldn't really pour my heart into them.

Every Labour Day weekend—Canadian holiday—my husband, his kids, and his friends go camping a few hours away. I had missed it the prior year (for the first time in eight years) because of my work schedule and I was excited that we could continue the tradition. That simple camping trip gave me the inspiration to turn freelancing into my chance to become an author.

I finally had a flexible schedule and a story to tell.

The idea came to me when I was sitting by the river reading *Committed* by Elizabeth Gilbert. I love her writing style and how she poured her life experiences onto the page. I knew there were many powerful insights hidden in my past, and that sharing my story could have an inspirational effect on others. The talented Elizabeth Gilbert gave me the inspiration to inspire others. I started writing *Dark Confessions of an Extraordinary, Ordinary Woman* the very same day that we came home from camping.

Four months into my home-based career and two weeks after we returned from camping, we decided to add a little extra work into my daily schedule. My husband had always wanted a dog, but I was not a dog person. I was afraid of big dogs and thought they were smelly, useless pets that we didn't need in our life.

Boy, was I wrong!

My husband found an ad online for an adorable puppy; it looked like a baby black bear. The picture made me melt. I agreed to meet the woman, who found the eight week old pup on her porch, and it was love at first sight. We named him Bruin and took him home immediately.

When I first held the fluffy, sweet-smelling ball of fur, I had no idea how much work was involved in caring for a puppy. Feeding and walking him was not a big problem, but puppies need to gnaw on something when their teeth are forming, and they are willing to use anything within reach as a chew toy. That includes my clothing, my shoes, and my ankles.

I'm a stepmom. I haven't experienced the time-consuming and patience-draining responsibilities of caring for a baby. I thought I would lose my mind after just a few days of caring for a small puppy. It's clear to me that I was never cut out to be a parent, which is a concept I will examine more thoroughly in a future book.

Our newest addition to the family interfered with my productivity. It was hard to get work done when I had a precious little puppy crawling across the keyboard. I was used to working on the laptop in my comfortable recliner. That was too accessible for my new companion, so I moved my work station to the kitchen table. Bruin didn't like it when the attention wasn't on him, so he'd nip at my ankles while I tried to type.

It didn't matter what Bruin did to distract, injure, or annoy me; I couldn't get mad at him. He was my baby, and I instantly knew I would always spoil him rotten. However, after about eight months of working late every night at home, because my new puppy was consuming my daytime working hours, I realized something had to change. That's when William suggested a second dog to keep the first one busy.

It made sense, right?

Bruin needed a playmate, and it couldn't continue to be me. I was struggling to finish enough work in a week to cover my bills. I spent several hours a day playing with my new fur-baby. A second dog would keep him occupied, so I could get more work done.

We told a few people we were considering adopting another dog (one old enough to be past the ankle-chewing stage) and my friend Shelley found the perfect match for Bruin online. He was a one-year-old lab mix named Thunder. Bruin loves all other dogs and we usually have a difficult time getting him to leave a dog park. He was overjoyed to have someone to constantly play with, and the two young pups were crazy for each other right from the start.

It was perfect timing, because my freelance business was starting to pick up again. I had a high online rating as a freelancer, I established several repeat clients, and even started writing for an American-based copy-writing company. The copywriting company, Quick Copy, seemed like the perfect opportunity for me. They dealt with the clients; all I had to do was write the ad copy, based on the instructions provided.

Quick Copy would give me new writing assignments each day with different due dates and pay rates. The pay varied based on the length and difficulty of the assignment. I still had the luxury of freelancing from home on my own schedule, plus I now had the stability of a steady income.

I experienced this career bliss for about six months, and then every aspect of my life went on hold. My Uncle Jeff had just come back from a vacation to Mexico and he had this undeniable gut feeling that something was wrong, so he stopped by the hospital for a few tests. He had been in remission for almost five months, and now all of a sudden the cancer was back.

This was the hardest part of the story for me to write and the section I didn't fill in until the very end. I remember every event from that week like it was yesterday, and my emotions are still as raw as when it first happened.

The first day I visited him, my uncle assured me he was fine and that he would beat the cancer once again. He explained to me that he was going to have a bone marrow transplant, to kill the cancer once and for all. My uncle still looked incredibly physically fit, so I trusted that he would be fine. We even made plans to run the Detroit half-marathon together in the fall. His last words before I left the hospital that night were:

"This is just a setback. I've got this, don't worry."

I'm sure he meant it when he said it, but God had a different plan. My uncle caught an infection, and his condition deteriorated drastically before I had a chance to return. He was on life support in less than a week. I was shocked by how different he looked the next time I saw him.

I had never seen my Uncle Jeff look frail and vulnerable. He was invincible in my eyes. He'd maintained a positive outlook and brave face throughout his first round of chemotherapy. This time he was clearly not doing well, and he couldn't hide his pain. The sight of him suffering left me shaken and scared.

His first battle with cancer lasted five months, and he looked physically strong through most of it. I could occasionally tell that he was tired or feeling weak, but his attitude and energy protected me from the severity of the situation. He was flirting with all the nurses and jogging laps around the hospital. I'd never let the thought of losing him slip into my head. I couldn't live in denial in anymore.

I stood there in disbelief as I listened to my father talk like my uncle's death was now suddenly inevitable. I didn't understand how things could change so radically, so quickly. My tactless father was already asking my uncle's friends if they knew where he kept his will.

My soul was still infused with the optimism my uncle had given me over the past year, so I left the hospital that night convinced that he would prove my father wrong. He was too mentally and physically strong to lose his battle to cancer. My Uncle Jeff was getting ready to retire and would finally be able to do whatever he wanted, whenever he wanted.

He couldn't die.

The universe couldn't be that cruel. My uncle's doctor appeared to agree with me, the following day. They gathered family and friends together to discuss the prognosis. The doctor told us that my uncle was physically healthy prior to the infection, and had a good chance of pulling through. He sounded quite hopeful and I felt reassured that my Uncle Jeff would be fine.

I left the hospital just after dinner, and told my father that I would go back at noon the following day. I asked him to please call me if anything changed with my uncle's condition. I didn't receive a call throughout the night, but woke up feeling like something wasn't right. I called my father's cellphone at ten o'clock the next morning, just to ease my worry..

"Have you been to the hospital yet."

"I'm here now. Uncle Jeff took a turn for the worse. You should come to the hospital as soon as possible."

"What?"

"We can talk more about it when you get here."

I don't know why my father didn't call me when he first learned that my uncle's condition had taken a turn for the worse. I didn't really give myself a chance to process what was happening. I quickly finished getting dressed and took off to the hospital. I saw my dad first; he greeted me with a long and silent hug.

I couldn't talk. I spent the next few hours listening to my family and my uncle's friends talk about him as if he was already gone. I could barely manage a nod. Nothing was making sense to me. How could he go from being strong and full of life to hopeless?

I wasn't ready to lose hope, but it wasn't up to me.

My father was convinced the only option was to end his life immediately, and his mind couldn't be changed. Arrangements were quickly made to take my uncle off of life support. We all crammed into his hospital room to witness my uncle's last breath within hours of reaching such a permanent conclusion. It happened so fast that it didn't seem real. He went on life support Friday night, and we took him off of it Sunday afternoon. I still don't understand, nor agree with, my father's hasty decision. It didn't matter. My uncle was gone, and I couldn't do anything to change it. In the blink of eye my invincible hero was permanently gone.

We spent the next few days truly celebrating my uncle's life. I've attended more funerals than I can remember, mostly in support of someone else's loss, but none were as positive and uplifting as my uncle's. Out of respect for his amazing attitude and the fact that he repeatedly vocalized his detest for traditional funerals, we only had a short, untraditional wake. My cousins and I wore bright, colorful party dresses and the funeral home was covered in cheerful photo displays that highlighted my uncle's zest for life. We did our best not to cry.

It took me weeks to absorb and accept the news, although I wouldn't say I've ever fully accepted my father's questionable choice. As awful as it sounds, I believe he rushed it for his own selfish reasons. Sadly, my father's behavior since my uncle's passing has reinforced that belief. It's the reason—or more accurately, one of many reasons—why the death of my uncle became the death of my relationship with my father.

It was also the slow and painful death of my freelance writing career. My downward slide started with being too distraught over the loss of my uncle to write anything required by my paying clientele, and ended when I became solely obsessed with working on my future novel.

No More Excuses

In an odd way that makes me feel guilty at times, my uncle's death finally gave me the freedom to live my life without hesitation. I have always worried about money. I've been responsible for my own expenses since I started college, and drowning in debt ever since. I am quite comfortable cutting corners, eating canned soup for dinner, and turning down vacations with friends. I was always the one who couldn't afford to go along with the group, and it didn't bother me, for the most part.

Still, I've missed two of my closest friend's weddings because they were destination weddings. I missed out on once-in-a-lifetime opportunities to go with my friend Taylor to visit our mutual friend while she was temporarily living in England, and then in Australia. I've missed out on a lot of amazing adventures and treasured memories as an adult, because I couldn't spare the funds to do so. My plans and dreams were always put on hold due to limited cash-flow. My most essential goal of my life was publishing the novel I started, but I hadn't invested enough time in it. It would take years to finish at my current rate of progress.

Thankfully, a sizeable inheritance from my Uncle Jeff finally gave me the financial security I needed to write my first book, *Dark Confessions of an Extraordinary, Ordinary Woman*. Just as importantly, it gave me the ability to say yes when I was invited to something new and exciting, regardless of the price tag. I could actually afford high-priced tickets to wine tours, fancy restaurants, and weekend getaways.

One of my favorite friends (I'm blessed with many), Paula, was enjoying her own new-found freedom as well and we became a lethal duo. She was a drop-dead gorgeous, highly successful, independent, and confident woman who was recently separated. She helped me celebrate my uncle's life the same way he lived it; without excuses, fear, or regret.

That summer turned the clock back twenty years. It was exactly what I needed to recover from what felt like a lifetime of overbearing bosses and office drama. I was technically still working, but I was only accepting a few hours of paid writing per day. I was living off the inheritance, and investing my working hours in finishing my book and scouting for potential publishers.

I became convinced that if I could publish a novel that benefited others, my uncle's death would not have been in vain. Uncle Jeff was a charitable man who donated regularly to the soup kitchens and shelters. He left the cancer ward at the hospital a significant chunk of money in his will. He was a selfless giver whom I admired and wanted to emulate. His life was stolen too quickly, and I felt the overwhelming urge to carry on his compassion for others in any little way that I could.

God gifted me with the ability to write. Although I had a clever way with catchy slogans that was no longer enough to feel satisfied. I had this overwhelming urge to use my writing to teach others how to truly love and appreciate their lives, flaws and all. I was starting to notice that our flaws are a big part of the fun in life, yet most people spend their lives trying to hide their imperfections.

I decided that writing the story of my failures and triumphs would become my first priority. I pulled my focus away from my new freelance career and stopped bidding on projects for new clients. I even let a few of my repeat clients go, because I wasn't able to keep up with their deadlines. I maintained three clients from my personal bidding and took on a few daily assignments from Quick Copy. I was certainly not earning enough to support myself, and the inheritance rapidly dwindled.

I'm a big believer that things happen for a reason. I search for explanations anytime my world takes a sudden twist or turn. For example, if I hadn't hit the career roadblock at Baumann's, I never would have ended up in an all-consuming hospitality management position that overwhelmed me. If my uncle wasn't diagnosed with Leukemia, I never would have quit that job to become a freelance writer. If he hadn't died so tragically young, I wouldn't have been able to afford the time that I needed to invest in *Dark Confessions of an Extraordinary, Ordinary Woman*.

It may be another cheesy cliché, but it's hard to deny that everything happens for a reason.

My life has been filled with unexpected disappointments and tragedies that led to incredible and rewarding opportunities. The same goes for my career as a home-based freelancer. It fell apart in the same unavoidable manner that it magically came together. I finished writing my book by the end of my summer of fun, and immediately sent it out to about a dozen different publishers. I looked specifically for publishers who specialized in books about female empowerment.

I was fortunate to find a great publisher quite quickly. I'd assumed it would take several months or years to find a company willing to take a chance on an unknown author. It only took a few weeks to get a response, and I ended up receiving several offers.

I'll be honest; I was stunned.

I think I'm a pretty good writer, but there are countless talented writers all over the world and very few of them find publishers. I have a few friends who have tried, with no luck. I wasn't expecting it to happen so quickly. In hindsight, it had to happen fast, because I was running out of money and my freelance career was suddenly tanking.

Quick Copy was managed by a young and inexperienced copywriter who didn't have the business skills to properly run it. On three different occasions, she had given me inaccurate or incomplete instructions and then begged me to rewrite the piece at no extra charge. I said yes the first two times it happened.

I wasn't as accommodating when it happened for a third time. The project was worth $220 and I already spent over twenty hours on it over the course of four days. The money wasn't worth my time, and the mistake meant that I would have to start from scratch. I told her that I would redo the assignment if she paid me an extra $140. I thought it was a reasonable compromise, but she disagreed and tried to force me into doing it for free. She threatened that I wouldn't get any future work and she would subtract the original $220 that I had been just paid off my next wire transfer if I didn't rewrite it based on the new instructions.

Somewhere between Baumann's and Quick Copy, my confidence had grown. I'd gained a backbone. I was no longer willing to be bullied, by anyone. I had completed the copy based on the instructions I was given, and I was not willing to fix someone else's mistake at my own expense. Unfortunately, taking that stand meant quitting Quick Copy. It's not a decision I regret even though it resulted in the end of my freelancing career as well.

I bid on a bunch of jobs promoted on the original freelance site I was using, but the average rates per article had dropped drastically. Word spinning software was gaining in popularity, and clients were no longer willing to pay $10 per 500 words. The going rate was now $5 per 500 words, and I only averaged about 1000 words per hour. I was too concerned with the quality of my writing to rush through it.

All of a sudden, I was averaging $150–$250 a week. The inheritance from my uncle was gone by mid-November. I was more frivolous than usual, but the money he generously gave me wasn't completely wasted. Some went on debt, some went into my retirement savings, and we used some of it to buy new windows for the house. Most importantly, I now had a publishing contract and a summer filled with incredible memories.

As per usual, all good things must come to end. After months of draining my savings and dipping into my credit, I knew it was time for me to return to the regular workforce. I went online and applied for every marketing or purchasing job I could find, which unfortunately was only three.

But I got lucky once again, because a friend from Baumann's who already knew my strong work ethic and bubbly personality was now working at a welding facility that was looking to hire a junior buyer. I had the experience they required, and a good connection to make the transition easier. I contacted my old friend, who responded with a glowing recommendation.

I was hired after three interviews, and scheduled to start the second week of January. It was a huge relief to start the new year with a steady income, even though it was hard to make the transition back to a full-time work schedule. I recognized that I had no choice but to make my new career opportunity work. My debt was just too high to survive, and I felt like I was a cat on her ninth life. God kept giving me fantastic opportunities, and I doubted he had any more miracle saves set aside for me. I had to make this job last until I could support myself as an author—a distant but doable dream.

The fact that my first book would be released in less than two months made it easier to close the door on my freelance career and re-enter the traditional workforce. My book's limitless potential left the door open to the life that I truly wanted. I was meant to be a real writer, not a copywriter promoting the latest products with slick sales pitches and cheesy slogans. I was always good at it, but it wasn't my real passion. I was now an author. There was no other job title I had ever coveted so deeply, and it was about to be my reality.

Finally On the Right Path

I was meant to write from my heart; to help others find comfort in the truth, to write powerful poetry, and tell stories with real purpose. My resume screamed purchasing and marketing professional, but that was not my destiny. It is merely the means I needed to cover my debt and daily expenses until I'm able to create a career as a full-time author.

My friends were already treating me like a successful author. They suggested a large book launch with dinner at a banquet hall, which I whittled down to a small gathering at my place with appetizers and my closest girlfriends. I was too worried that they wouldn't get the RSVP's they expected.

Not everyone was thrilled about the release of my first book, for various reasons, and I was lacking support from people whom I can usually count on. I felt more secure keeping the invite list to only those people I knew were sincerely excited about my story being shared with the world.

We had a fabulous evening celebrating the book and each other. Every friend who attended my book release has been a vital source of support, marketing help, and positive energy since its launch. They were all necessary fuel for my journey, and I am sincerely grateful.

My new company was also very supportive of my extracurricular activities. They were delighted to have an author on their staff. The vice president and president of the company, as well as countless others, were kind enough to buy a copy from me.

My new job had many good points, but I knew it wasn't something I could do for the rest of my life. I needed to do everything I could to promote *Dark Confessions of an Extraordinary, Ordinary Woman*, to ensure I had the financial means to return to writing full-time. I spent my days purchasing consumables and tools for the welding facility, and my evenings aggressively promoting my first book on Facebook and Twitter. I was convinced that I was destined to be a writer, and my goal was to reach a level where I could live off my novels by the time I reached age fifty. That meant fifteen more years at the welding facility.

I had a new fifteen year plan for my life!

My plan would require a major commitment, a lot of writing, and a bit of luck. Success was not guaranteed, even if I did everything right. I would need to make a massive investment in my dream without any certainty of reward. Every successful person once defied the odds and risked their time and money without any reassurance that it would ever be repaid. I had to look past my fear that it would be a failure, and believe in it enthusiastically.

The initial reviews were all quite positive, but they were mostly people who knew me personally. Some strangers who enjoyed my story sent me private messages, since the subject matter is a sensitive issue to the majority of the women who would benefit from reading it. In the first month, I sold about 150 copies locally. I didn't have any idea if people were buying it online.

I've never experienced such a drastic mix of emotions as I did when I waited months to find out my book sales. I was anxious, discouraged, doubtful, excited, obsessed, and nauseous. I'm pretty sure I drove my closest friends crazy. My publisher would slowly release disappointing sales figures that left me wondering if my book would ever gain the recognition I needed to try again. I'd promised people that there would be a second book, and now I was questioning if my writing talent was as good as I thought.

Was my ego greater than my talent?

I must admit that I wasted several months debating whether or not I should write a second book. A few of my friends would inquire on its progress, and I would be forced to confess I'd only finished a few pages. I knew the subject matter of my second book could hinder future employment opportunities, and it was becoming glaringly obvious that my first book wasn't going to provide me any financial security anytime soon. I planned on publishing a book called *Dirty Secrets of the World's Worst Employee*, and I doubted it would be a beneficial credit on my resume.

I finally forced myself to invest some time on my second book in the middle of April, after hearing several positive reviews in a row. It was my fake it 'til you make it philosophy. I had to act like I was certain of the book's success, despite the declining local sales and falling online rankings. I knew there was still hope for its success, as long it was inspiring the people who were reading it.

Reflecting back on it, my goal was to help others see their own worth and I was achieving that. It was foolish of me to assume that my book would be an instant hit, and it was that self-centric mindset that caused me to temporarily lose focus of my goal's true purpose.

My expectations of what I could accomplish with my first book were significantly greater than reality, but I was still successful. I had to reprogram my mindset to be happy with what I was doing instead of insisting I could be doing more. I wasn't failing. Achieving my dream career was a work in progress.

My triumph over a failed relationship and depression wasn't the only lesson I could pass on to others, and I couldn't give up on yet another fifteen year plan. My objective was to spend my life writing books that made people feel better about themselves. It was a goal I'd dedicated to my uncle, and I would not allow myself to stop my pursuit of it.

The need to chase that dream of becoming a career author became increasingly important after an incident at the welding facility that left a familiar pain in my stomach. A narcissistic bully threatened and cornered a co-worker.

I was aware of an ongoing feud between my department and the company's maintenance team, but I never imagine it would escalate to the extent of actual anger. We discovered questionable charges from one of maintenance team's preferred suppliers, and decided to bring the company's owner in to further investigate their business practices. We didn't have enough evidence to actively pursue our suspicions without starting an internal war, so the meeting was strictly to get to know the supplier better.

Unfortunately, the meeting never took place.

A different member of the maintenance team intercepted the supplier the moment he walked in the front door. We saw the maintenance supervisor lingering in the lobby prior to the meeting time, but we didn't know he was with the supplier until almost an hour later.

Andrew, another junior buyer in my department, waited for almost an hour and then sent the supplier a harsh email expressing his frustration with being stood up. The supplier called to apologize, but the buyer was unforgiving.

Andrew screamed into the phone, "You have disrespected me and my boss. The relationship is damaged," before slamming the phone back into the receiver.

The largest and toughest of the maintenance men, Roy, arrived at the entranceway to our department within ten minutes of the buyer ending that phone call. I could tell he was angry. His cheeks were flushed, and he had an intense look in his eyes.

"Andrew, can I see you over here?"

I shouldn't use a question mark, since Roy wasn't asking a question. The tone of his voice sounded more like a command. It was a frightening command, but Andrew followed without hesitation. Andrew was a well-liked and charming guy. He felt confident he could calm the beast without incident.

As Roy approached Andrew, I head Roy snap at him. "You want to see respect? I'll show you respect."

The pair disappeared into the kitchenette just outside the entrance to our department. I told my boss what Roy had said, and she suggested I bring HR up there immediately. As I walked past the kitchenette to get the HR manager, I glanced over my shoulder to see what was going on inside. I could see that the maintenance man had his hand on the kitchen counter and was inches away from Andrew's face, whispering threats about not messing with his suppliers.

While I was getting the HR manager, my boss grabbed the attention of the closest male in our department, another senior manager. She was smart and knew better than to approach the situation alone. When I arrived at the opening to the kitchenette, my boss and the other manager were asking Roy to back off. The HR manager joined in, but was quickly shoved out of the way, so Roy could close the door to the small room. My boss and the two managers were on the outside, while the irate maintenance supervisor and young buyer were inside.

I was sincerely worried about what was happening on the other side of that door. It brought back many painful memories from my past relationship, and I started to imagine the worst-case scenario.

No one ended up getting hurt, but it showed me that my new job had some of the same flaws as previous places of employment. Threats and intimidation appear to be quite prevalent in every workplace.

My first instinct was to find a new job, and I didn't have to look too hard for a wide range of viable options. In fact, I randomly received an email about a potential job the day after the incident. I scheduled the interview and started to prepare myself for my next adventure. I thought maybe it was fate, telling me it was time to move on.

I honestly hated the thought of starting over again so soon, but I couldn't work at a company that would allow an employee to be treated so poorly. Roy wasn't fired, and no one in management took the incident very seriously. I was fighting against injustices, bullying, and narcissistic intimidation online to promote my first book; how could I work for a company that turned a blind eye to an obvious violation of a person's rights?

However, I was bullied out of a job I loved when I was at the department store. I was not going to let it happen again. I thoroughly enjoyed working with almost all of my coworkers, the maintenance man excluded, and this was the only time the company had disappointed me.

I made the choice to stick it out at the welding facility. I prayed justice would be served in good time, and unlike the department store, it actually happened. It took nine months and several other incidents of destructive and narcissistic behavior, but the maintenance man was finally fired.

In an odd coincidence, he was fired within twenty-four hours of catching him lying in an email I initiated. Managers were copied on the email, and his response to my original message was aggressive and intentionally confrontational. I know it wasn't the reason he was fired the next day, but I'm sure it didn't help his case.

Reflecting back on my career, it's obvious that every job has its drawbacks and most managers don't want to deal with problems if they can be neatly swept under a rug and forgotten. It didn't mean I was working for a bad company. It's the same story everywhere. You have to take the good with the bad in all aspects of life.

One of the worthwhile benefits of my new place of employment was the senior buyer. She was everything I hoped Agnes would be. She was a strong and confident woman who was thrilled to pass on her experience to her staff. She encouraged me to speak up for myself, taught me effective negotiation techniques, and empowered me to take ownership of special projects and challenging tasks. She also repeatedly praised my accuracy, critical thinking, and communication skills. My new manager has rebuilt what Agnes tore down.

The company itself did an excellent job of showing their appreciation as well. Within the first year of working there, I was given a winter coat, four golf shirts, two t-shirts, a hat, gift cards to the mall, and countless free lunches and dinners. The executives, as well as my manager, made a point of rewarding hard work. It wasn't always an easy environment to work in, but I was compensated well for any stress or conflicts I endured.

Chasing My Dream
with Enthusiasm

When I finally made the brave decision to publish the professional side of my life story, I decided to give Sean, the owner at the department store, one more chance to do the right thing. I had been working on writing this book relentlessly for several weeks in a row. It was turning out better than I imagined, if I do say so myself.

The only former colleague that I felt bad writing about was the president of Baumann's, because of how he looked in my story. I felt sorry for him, and didn't want my story to have a negative impact on his livelihood. I also wanted to show my current fans—domestic violence survivors—that speaking up can create change. I needed Sean Baumann to listen to me and finally do something to right the wrong. That type of response would give me the perfect fairytale ending to the story of my crooked career path.

So, I sent him another email.

> Good Morning Sean,
>
> I am sure you didn't expect to hear from me after so much time has gone by, but I felt it was only fair to give you a heads up about what I am working on. I am writing my second novel, *Dirty Secrets of the World's Worst Employee*, and my current publisher has agreed to publish it in the fall of 2015. The title is satirical and obviously does not reflect the type of employee I am. However, the book will cover my entire career history in

detail, and the greatest focus will be on my experiences at Baumann's. I only refer to it as "family department store," but it won't be hard to figure out for anyone who knows me personally.

I saved all of the critical and damaging information from when I worked there and included an exact copy of the letter I sent you and Ryan after I left. I also included our email correspondence from after I left and my conversations with former employees. Every detail of the mistreatment of employees will be in the book, and I have evidence to prove pretty much all of it.

My first novel is already a success; I've sold over 400 copies since it was released in March of 2014. That's impressive for a local author. My *Dark Confession of an Extraordinary, Ordinary Woman* page on Facebook has almost 3,000 followers, and my Twitter account @AuthorJennSadai has almost 400 followers. I've received numerous messages from people who can't wait to read my next book, especially every current and former Baumann's employee. I am quickly making a name for myself as an author, and my popularity grows daily. I will begin promoting *Dirty Secrets of the World's Worst Employee* using social media in the new year.

I am contacting you to give you one last chance to fix the ending to this story. I know you want to do the right thing, but it is out of your control. One of my sources told me you said, "Your father set you up to fail by leaving you with her." This is your chance to succeed despite her obvious blackmail. Use the labor laws and Bill 168 to remove the cancer from your business before it goes public. I won't be submitting the final draft of the story until sometime in March. There is still time to edit it. I have a sincere affection for Baumann's and 98% of its employees. I would hate to damage the company's reputation or my friend's careers if it can be helped.

Please contact me if you plan on resolving your problem before March. If I don't hear from you, I'll assume you are fine with the truth being published as it stands now.

Thank you sincerely,

Jenn

A month went by of energetically working on this story without receiving a response. I assumed he either didn't read it, or he wasn't worried about the content of my book. I am often underestimated. It would be almost unfathomable to Sean that I'd have the courage to put Agnes' mistakes in print. She was feared by nearly everyone at the department store, including the owners.

That was the false sense of security I had lured myself into until a registered letter arrived in the mail. It was a letter from Sean Baumann threatening that I would be personally sued if I published anything defamatory about the company. I had already decided to conceal everyone's identity and to take any measures necessary to protect the other characters from my sordid career history. I was doing so partially out of respect for the innocent, as well as to avoid being sued. I can't afford a lawsuit and don't want one. I wasn't trying to start a war: I was simply trying to stop a tyrant. I wanted to show the world that David could still slay Goliath.

Instead, I opened the door to a lawsuit. I decided to be extra cautious and allow my former employer a first peek at *Dirty Secrets of the World's Worst Employee* to ensure I wouldn't be sued later on. Maybe if he read the story, he would realize the truth and allow me to share my story with others who have faced similar struggles. I no longer believed that I could change the way he ran the business, but I still believed he was a good person stuck in a bad situation.

This was my response to the letter threatening legal action:

> Sean,
> I can't accurately express how sincerely sad your registered letter made me. For some reason, I still had respect for you and believed you knew the truth. However, I already sought legal advice and made some necessary changes to protect myself and your store. I changed it to a department store, changed physical descriptions, name of the store, and job titles. I plan on removing my past employment history from LinkedIn before publishing. I can't help the people who know me and know where I worked, but I've personally told most of them the truth already.

As for the blackmail comment, how else could a "family" store let someone bully and mistreat people without any repercussion? Blackmail was the only thing that made sense of how you would allow employee after employee to be forced out by her, but I can delete that paragraph if it prevents a lawsuit. I'll also let you read it once I'm done, before it's published. I still have physical proof of everything that happened to me. You can ask for proof of anything in the story relating to the "department store" that you don't believe. The only rule is that if I can prove it's true, it will stay in the book—and you can't sue me over it. You can also ask me to make other changes to insignificant details to further hide your store's identity.

I respect that you need to protect your store's reputation. Too many of my friends (people I genuinely love) still work there, and I wouldn't want to destroy their careers. I meant it when I wrote, "I would hate to damage the company's reputation or my friend's careers if it can be helped." The fact that you don't believe me shows that you don't know me at all. All I want is to offer some justice to those who were treated so poorly. They'll know who it's about, and will appreciate seeing the truth in print. It's for the victims, and for anyone else who has questioned their self-worth because of a bully.

Wait until you read the book before you plan a lawsuit. At that time, we can discuss how to free the truth without destroying what your family has built. It is truly disappointing that your first response is to sue. When you and I talked on the phone about how Helen, Deanna, and I were treated, I actually believed you cared. I wish I hadn't been wrong.

Sincerely,

Jenn

I am now a brave woman, sometimes too brave. When I'm fighting injustices, I feel invincible. I would like to believe that as long as I am being honest and fair, I will be protected from prosecution. However, reality doesn't always mimic my ideals. Sean obviously felt that I was out to destroy his company, and he was willing to go to any measure to stop me. I thought he was compassionate and that he knew me better than that. To my surprise, he actually responded to that email with another threatening letter directly from his lawyer.

Sean Baumann was not the first person to disappoint me. I have a tendency to believe the best in everyone. It doesn't always work out the way I hope, but I refuse to change this character trait. I'd rather assume that most people try to do what's right, and don't want to inflict any suffering on others. I just wish people would assume the best about me.

Although I've made many fundamental mistakes over my crazy career, my intentions have never been to harm anyone or any company. Even when everything went sour at Baumann's, I didn't sue the company for wrongful dismissal like other former employees. I worked hard, and still did my best even after I found out I no longer had a job there.

That's just who I am, and I'm proud of it.

I can admit now that Agnes was right about me to some degree, and I don't hold what happened to me against her. Yes, the review she manufactured was completely inaccurate. She is a bully, and she was wrong about how beneficial I would have been in an art director position. I've proven my marketing skills with my ability to build my own personal brand.

However, I was also responsible because I didn't stick up for myself when it happened. I allowed her to chip away at my self-esteem and make me question my own worthiness. I didn't gain the self-confidence I have now until long after I was forced to leave that job. Agnes mainly thought I wasn't worthy of working at the department store because I was too soft-hearted. She wasn't really wrong about that.

I struggled to fire a waitress whom we caught stealing when I was a manager at the golf course. I never would have survived as a director at the department store under her leadership. I was more of a cheerleader than a leader. I've gained a backbone since then, but I still can't be cutthroat or heartless in any situation. I can, however, be tough and firm when it's necessary; significant progress from the old me.

My crooked career path has taught me a lot about myself and human nature. Most people try to do the *right* thing, but many can easily be swayed to choose the most *convenient* thing, the most *profitable* thing, or the most *self-serving* thing instead.

Our first priority should be to protect our own best interests. In some instances, that will create an ethical gray area. The line that divides the ethical and immoral choices in our careers is the impact our decisions have on others. Everyone else is trying to survive their own professional journey, and the goal should never be to make theirs more difficult.

There are actually quite a few fundamental life lessons I've learned from my unpredictable career history. One of the most obvious, to anyone who has had multiple places of employment, is that every company has its dirty secrets. Whether it is an unscrupulous owner, an unreasonable boss, or crazy coworkers, there is always something scandalous going on behind the scenes. Switching jobs won't solve the problem.

It's all about perspective.

Every day I come home to my loving husband and excessively affectionate dogs. I spend my weekends writing, running, and socializing with my wonderful family and friends. It doesn't matter where I'm earning my living. My real life exists in those precious hours after I punch out. Those are the moments that make me whole.

Another valuable insight I've gained over the course of my career is to not allow others to dictate my self-worth. I'm a good employee, sometimes great. I care about the companies I work for, even when they don't show sincere concern for me. I'm smart and capable. Any employer would be lucky to have me. If an insecure manager or a sexist boss doesn't appreciate what I have to offer, then it's their loss.

That was a hard lesson for someone who tends to already be pretty hard on herself, which is a trait I share with many women. Women are more likely to fall victim to irrational insecurities, because they feel a greater pressure when it comes to proving themselves.

I've noticed as well that most women have a harder time saying no, in both their personal and professional lives. This is why women usually end up carrying a larger percentage of the workload. Sorry guys, but I've seen this over and over again in my career.

The few women I've met who have worked their way to the top and have the guts to delegate are usually a lot tougher to deal with than men in similar power positions. They tend to be more destructive and demanding, sometimes demeaning, and even deceptive. They often have the reputation of being a bitch, and are disliked by most co-workers.

Is that the only way they can be heard and taken seriously?

Did my old boss at Baumann's have to behave that way, in order to rise to the top?

Agnes would have started her career at the beginning of the women's movement. Thirty years ago, women had to loudly bust down barriers and insist on equality to be given a chance. It is getting better for women in the workplace, but there still isn't job equality. Women are usually paid less for equivalent positions, and are often overlooked for promotions because they are either too aggressive or too meek.

I've only met one female boss who has somewhat mastered the art of give and take, and even she struggles to be heard by men in power. My current boss at the welding facility knows when to be tough and how to use her voice to get things done. She uses honesty and passion to convey her issues and ideas. When all else fails, she finds one man who supports her initiative and engages his voice to back her own.

It's sad, but true. Very few men will give female co-workers the same respect they give their male counterparts. My vocal manager is often mistaken for dramatic, emotional, or aggressive, but I've seen the truth. No one listens to her until she makes a huge fuss about it. The male executives have driven her to extremes.

Most men have no clue that their behavior is disrespectful and sexist. Over the past twenty years in the workforce—holy cow I'm really that old—I've seen and heard it all. Seemingly sweet men will let an inappropriate comment slip, proving undeniably that they don't consider their female co-workers as equals. The comments I've overheard in my career are probably not surprising to most female professionals.

"Darling, can you take the meeting minutes?"

It's not my meeting. I'm not the junior employee in the room. But since I'm the only female in the room, therefore that duty falls on me.

"Good morning beautiful! I was wondering, could you arrange lunch for today's meeting?"

First, I don't call you handsome, so why do you feel the need to address me with your assessment of my physical appearance? Also, why is your time more valuable than mine? You're not my superior, manager, or boss, yet you pass off every menial task to me.

What's worse is when a male co-worker or manager misinterprets your positive attitude and enthusiasm as an open invitation for a more personal relationship. This happened to me at several jobs, especially in the hospitality industry. However, it is definitely not limited to the food service positions. I have a friend in a managerial role at a financial institution who was harassed on a regular basis by her direct superior.

I'll share her story because it is the most graphic example of how many business men view their female colleagues. My friend's boss viewed her greatest assets to be her large breasts and voluptuous physique. He repeatedly commented on his desire to see her breasts, and would often comment on their perkiness. He even told her how he pleasured himself, while thinking about her body.

His dirty texts and suggestive remarks made her uncomfortable, but she never did anything about it. He rewarded her silence with promotions, bonuses, and raises. She was finally able to move around in the company and get away from him.

She's not alone. I've witnessed a female manager fondled by a client, waitresses groped by overly-friendly patrons, and male co-workers blatantly leering and objectifying females in the office. When these problems are brought to the attention of leaders in the company, which are usually male, these women are twisted into being the provoker of the incident rather than the victim.

"You were flirting with him too."

"You must have liked it, if you didn't tell him to stop."

"You should expect that response when you dress like that."

Men's inability to control their hormones has always been a women's issue. Now, this book's intent is not to bash male behavior. I merely feel the need to highlight the issue. I view everything I publish as a global platform I can use to address problems many people are facing. I have a voice now, and I'm not afraid to use it.

Thanks to my empowering friend who convinced me that I could finish a marathon, the self-esteem boost I got from publishing my first book, and my new boss's fantastic example, I am finally starting to excel at speaking up and being heard.

Up until recently, I've had very few of my co-workers and managers take me seriously, because I am obedient and submissive. I do what is asked of me without argument. Sometimes I make suggestions for improvement, but if a suggestion is not embraced by a manager, I let it go.

That was the old me. I'm more passionate now and my new boss not only supports my ideas, she encourages them whole-heartedly. Although I don't plan on buying welding supplies for the rest of my life, and sincerely pray that I will one day support myself as an author, it's a pretty decent job. I've experienced enough troubles in my work history to recognize when I've found something worth keeping.

Hopefully nothing tragic or unexpected will happen with my new job before I'm able to commit fully to my dream of becoming an author. If my crooked career history has taught me anything, it's that a seemingly great job can quickly turn upside down without warning. If that happens, at least I'm pretty confident that I will land on my feet. I always do.

Regardless of the type of employee you are or where you work, there will always be obstacles. You can either face them and keep moving forward, or let them take you down. Just remember it isn't what you do to earn a living that defines who you are in this world. It's how you live your life that makes up your true character.

The last lesson I learned holds my dirtiest secret. I am so embarrassed by this secret that I kept it from everyone, including my closest confidant, Rachel. My first book, *Dark Confessions of an Extraordinary, Ordinary Woman* hasn't really taken off. I'd experienced some false hope a few months before publishing it, which inspired me to finally finish my second book— the one you're almost finished reading.

I was checking a website daily that showed every time my barcode was scanned. It was showing that my book's barcode had been scanned almost every other day. I compared it with the websites that allowed me to verify sales and each scan appeared to match up with a book sale. The following month, it increased to a new scan every day. My publisher thought the same thing might be possible, but hadn't exactly confirmed my findings.

I didn't care. My book was finally selling, and I was overjoyed. I told everyone. Well, now I'm using this book to tell everyone I was wrong. I found out that at least half of those scans were only sites updating their prices. I had sold almost four hundred books, instead of the well over five hundred copies I had originally estimated. I only sold six copies in March, so sales were declining again.

My first book hasn't exactly been profitable. I invested a dozen or more hours a week for a year writing it, and then the same amount of time the following year promoting it, as well as female empowerment and domestic violence awareness on social media. I've profited a few hundred dollars off of my books over the last two years.

If I sound like I'm complaining, I'm definitely not. My first book was a huge success in my eyes. Only four hundred people may have read my story, but over a hundred of those readers have contacted me out of appreciation. My story has opened up necessary dialogues, built new friendships, and ended toxic relationships.

My goal was to have a positive effect on the world. I needed to do something meaningful with my life and I'm confident I've achieved what I intended. Every person I help only inspires me to do more. I want to continue to write stories that remind us it's okay to have flaws. There is no shame in owning up to your career and relationship mistakes.

We're not perfect, and that's okay.

My imperfections helped me discover my talent and my purpose. They gave me an interesting story to tell and advice worthy of sharing. The world is filled with passionate people who are proactively pursuing their purpose, all of whom are flawed. Never let self-doubt or the fear of failure stop you from chasing your dreams with enthusiasm. You only fail when you stop trying. I have no intention on stopping.

Live a limitless life.

Crooked Path

By Jenn Sadai

This is your life; your journey.
You decide the route you take.
Determine where you want to go.
Plan for the life you hope to make.

You control the effort you put in.
But, not everything will go your way.
You don't control circumstance.
'Cause every traveler has their say.

Life doesn't follow a straight path.
It weaves in and out of those passing by.
There are sudden dips and hurdles.
That will teach you how to fly.

Crazy twists and turns throughout
Moments that make you want to quit.
No matter where your crooked path goes.
You're stronger for having followed it.

About the Author

Jenn Sadai always knew she wanted to be a writer. She started writing poetry in elementary school and published her first short story when she was only thirteen years old. Unfortunately, unexpected responsibilities and significant debt knocked her off course before she really began. It wasn't until someone she loved was faced with a terminal illness that she decided to risk it all and pursue her dream of becoming a published author. This leap of faith resulted in her first book, *Dark Confessions of an Extraordinary, Ordinary Woman*, which was released in February of 2014. Her second book, *Dirty Secrets of the World's Worst Employee*, delves into Jenn's crooked career path and the various roles she filled before returning to her true calling. Jenn Sadai was born in Windsor, Ontario, where she still resides with her loving husband, four fantastic stepchildren, and two loveable labs. She is an avid runner who has finished two full marathons and five half-marathons. Jenn Sadai is a strong believer that anything in life is possible when you make your goals a priority.

Jenn Sadai is currently working on her first fictional story, as well as another memoir, *Cottage Cheese Thighs*, that will examine her never-ending struggle with her weight, body image, and self-esteem.

CPSIA information can be obtained
at www.ICGtesting.com
Printed in the USA
FFOW05n0409021015

9 781939 289711